# Agile Extension to the BABOK® Guide

v2

IIBA® International Institute
of Business Analysis™

# Table of Contents

# Chapter 4: Strategy Horizon

# Chapter 5: Initiative Horizon

# Chapter 6: Delivery Horizon

# Chapter 7: Techniques

# 1 Introduction

## 1.1 Purpose of the Agile Extension to the BABOK® Guide

Agile methods and approaches have become prevalent in recent years. The ideas which were identified in the realm of software product development have spread beyond software development into many other areas that are impacted by business analysis. This means that the practice of business analysis has to evolve to support the new ways of working, not just in software development but in any area of the business where change is happening rapidly. In this context, the term agile refers to a mindset or way of thinking about work. Agile is not a specific set of practices or techniques.

The *Agile Extension to the BABOK® Guide* (*Agile Extension*) version 2 is the leading guide for describing the benefits, activities, tasks, skills, and practices required for effective business analysis with an agile mindset which has a constant focus on delivering business value. It also describes how techniques and concepts commonly used in agile approaches can be applied to business analysis practices. The *Agile Extension* version 2 provides practitioners, teams, and organizations a base of knowledge to enable effective agile business analysis in order to generate successful business outcomes that add real business and customer value.

### 1.1.1 Why Version 2?

Since version 1 of the *Agile Extension* was released, the state of practice has advanced. Version 2 of the *Agile Extension* taps into the latest thinking and presents ideas and techniques representing good agile business analysis practices.

The primary purpose of the *Agile Extension* version 2 is to describe the link between business analysis practices applied with an agile mindset, defined here as agile business analysis, and *A Guide to the Business Analysis Body of Knowledge*® (*BABOK*® *Guide* ) version 3. *BABOK*® *Guide* version 3 reflects the evolution of the business analysis discipline and its most common practices, and this *Agile Extension* version 2 demonstrates the evolution of agile business analysis practices and common techniques.

The *Agile Extension* introduces a multi-level, rolling planning model to help practitioners, teams, and organizations manage business analysis work, so they can quickly leverage learning and discover what provides the most actual value. This rolling wave planning model is presented using three horizons which provide context and scope for lower levels. The three horizons are: the Strategy Horizon, the Initiative Horizon, and the Delivery Horizon.

There are a wide variety of techniques, processes, and tools that can be applied to agile business analysis. There is no single approach that should be applied to every context, and part of the skill of the agile business analysis practitioner is to select the most effective techniques for the specific context; the *Agile Extension* does provide some advice for practitioners on the applicability of different techniques to different contexts.

## 1.2 What is Agile Business Analysis?

Agile business analysis is the practice of business analysis in an agile context with an agile mindset. Agile business analysis can provide a competitive advantage in fast-paced and complex environments and has moved beyond software development initiatives to any business domain. Organizations have adopted agile practices at all levels of planning and in many diverse business areas.

A key element of the agile mindset is inspecting and adapting. Feedback at one horizon influences decisions at all the horizons which results in changes to work at the horizons. For more detailed information on horizons, see 3. Analysis at Multiple Horizons, 4. Strategy Horizon, 5. Initiative Horizon, and 6. Delivery Horizon.

**Figure 1.2.1: Agile Business Analysis**

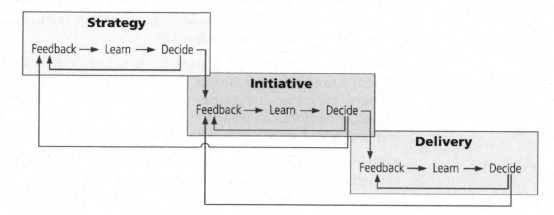

Agile business analysis focuses on maximizing business value. This constant focus on business value produces better and more timely business outcomes.

### 1.2.1          About Agile Delivery

Agile delivery is a business strategy that creates value through fast feedback and short decision cycles. The agile analysis mindset is based on the Agile Manifesto and the Principles of Agile Business Analysis (for more information, see 2.6. Principles of Agile Business Analysis)

Agile delivery planning takes two primary forms: iterative and adaptive.

- Iterative planning prioritizes and refines the work in short cycles designed to provide focus and increase the feedback and learning gained from stakeholders.

- Adaptive planning involves the continuous change to long-term plans. Constant planning and analysis is used to prioritize and refine the work to be done to deliver the highest value.

Agile approaches deliver value incrementally, slicing the product into small pieces, prioritizing them by business value, and delivering new items of value frequently. Incremental delivery allows for rapid feedback, learning, and adapting to change.

The *Agile Extension to the BABOK® Guide* is agnostic to the approach used and provides benefits, activities, tasks, skills, practices, and techniques applicable to any agile approach. There is no "one size fits all" approach and techniques from both planning approaches can be used together.

### 1.2.2          Business Analysis in the Organization

Business analysis is fundamental to organizations striving to deliver value to their customers. Agile business analysis uses continuous feedback and learning to prioritize delivery, minimize waste, and increase customer value.

Organizations gain feedback from a number of sources such as customers, competitors, partners, investors, subject matter experts, and regulators. Feedback collected can be used to help organizations understand if they are delivering the value customers want. Organizations continually learn what works in their environment. Rapid change means organizations need to identify, collect, and process stakeholder feedback quicker.

Feedback is used to prioritize work items based on those that deliver the most value and to eliminate those that do not. Agile business analysis uses this feedback to effectively create and distribute value. It helps individuals, teams, and organizations focus on what delivers the most value. Part of this focus includes identifying and avoiding work that does not deliver the value sought.

Agile business analysis techniques help organizations interpret the constant flow of feedback and learning in order to prioritize work with enough speed to meet stakeholder needs, take advantage of opportunities, and respond to change.

Agile product delivery, whether for external or internal stakeholders, includes a degree of uncertainty. By delivering value in a minimum viable way as early as possible, organizations can learn what is valuable and what is not, and help to minimize waste and understand what value meets stakeholders' needs.

### 1.2.3　Agile Business Analysis for Practitioners

Business analysis practitioners use agile business analysis techniques to maximize business value, to rapidly learn, adapt and respond to change, and to reduce waste by maximizing the amount of work not done.

Agile business analysis practitioners use learning derived from stakeholder feedback in order to guide the delivery process and deliver value constantly. Agile business analysis activities play a central role in learning and identifying what is truly valuable, what does not add value, and facilitate the learning and communication needed to continually deliver the right value.

Agile business analysis activities

- provide the link between the organization's strategy and the initiatives resourced to meet the goals of the strategy,
- discover, interpret, and communicate information in order to increase understanding and clarity on where value can be created,
- clarify for whom value is created, who can contribute to the creation of value, and who else might be impacted, and
- help stakeholders make decisions about approaches, priorities, and trade-offs to stay focused on continuous value creation in the face of constraints, differing opinions, risks, and complexity.

Agile business analysis supports an environment of creativity, rapid learning, and experimentation which leads to innovation.

There are seven principles of agile analysis that guide agile business analysis practitioners:

- See the Whole

- Think as a Customer

- Analyze to Determine What is Valuable

- Get Real Using Examples:

- Understand What is Doable

- Stimulate Collaboration and Continuous Improvement

- Avoid Waste

For more information regarding these seven principles, see 2.6. Principles of Agile Business Analysis.

### 1.2.4    Three Horizons of Agile Business Analysis

A key concept in the *Agile Extension* is planning horizons. A planning horizon represents a view of work within an organization with a level of granularity appropriate to the time frame being planned for and the nature of the feedback loops used. The *Agile Extension* defines three horizons: Strategy (see 4. Strategy Horizon), Initiative (see 5. Initiative Horizon), and Delivery (see 6. Delivery Horizon). This framework provides a model to describe agile business analysis. Individual practitioners and organizations may employ different terms, levels of granularity, and time frames based on the context of the organization and the work being done.

Each horizon uses different time spans and level of detail, and the *Agile Extension* explores agile business analysis techniques and practices used at each horizon to deliver business value. The specific time spans for each horizon differ from organization to organization but the concept of planning at multiple time horizons and different levels of granularity is central to agile business analysis.

The Strategy Horizon looks at all of the work being undertaken in an organization and is used to make decisions at the highest levels about what work should be funded, the approaches to be taken, the availability of skills and resources, and alignment with business goals. The level of granularity is about selecting which initiatives should be undertaken, how they will be funded, and how they will be monitored. Feedback is based on assessing how well business goals are being met.

The Initiative Horizon looks at the work needed to produce a single product, either for internal use in the organization or customer facing. Each initiative should have clear goals which help to achieve specific strategic outcomes. The level of granularity is related to the specific features the product will have and how these are divided into discrete pieces of business value. Feedback is based on customer or user interaction with the product and value delivered.

The Delivery Horizon is where work happens: implementation teams build discrete pieces of the product using iterative or adaptive and incremental techniques, working from a prioritized list based on business value as identified at the Initiative and Strategy Horizons.

## 1.3 Structure

The core content of the *Agile Extension* is the Strategy, Initiative, and Delivery Horizons. These chapters describe common agile business analysis practices.

The chapters on The Agile Mindset, Analysis at Multiple Horizons, and Techniques form the extended content in the *Agile Extension*. These chapters provide a richer understanding and context to agile business analysis activities.

The Appendices of the *Agile Extension* include the Glossary, Mapping *BABOK® Guide* Tasks to Horizons, Contributors, Contributors, and a Summary of Changes from Agile Extension to the *BABOK® Guide* version 1.

# 2 The Agile Mindset

Agile is best described as a mindset that guides the way work is approached. Agile is not a methodology that prescribes how to do that work.

Agile business analysis is comprised of applying an agile mindset to the fundamental knowledge, competencies, and techniques of business analysis. Appendix B: Mapping BABOK Guide Tasks to Horizons demonstrates how an agile mindset can be applied to each *BABOK® Guide* task.

An agile mindset drives agile business analysis practitioners' thinking and behaviour. This, combined with a set of practices and techniques which enable effective delivery of just enough of the right product to the right people early and often, and the focus on maximizing value, are the goals of agile business analysis.

The goal of applying an agile mindset is to maximize the outcome (value delivered) with minimum output: "do less and do the right things, right".

## 2.1 What is an Agile Mindset?

The agile mindset is based on a common core of human values that include respect, courage, collaboration, continuous learning, customer focus, and value maximization. These values find their clearest expression in the Manifesto for Agile Software Development (Agile Manifesto).

The main aspects of an agile mindset include

- deliver value rapidly and consistently,
- collaborate courageously,

- iterate to learn,

- simplify to avoid waste,

- consider context and adapt to realities,

- reflect on feedback and adapt both product and process, and

- produce the highest quality products.

## 2.2 The Agile Mindset, Methodologies, and Frameworks

Agile is best described as a mindset because the values and subsequent principles explain ideas and attitudes with which people approach a situation, but do not prescribe exactly what they do in those situations.

Every situation is unique – there is no single "agile" approach. There are a variety of techniques, processes, and tools which can be applied in different combinations to different extents depending on the context. Agile teams are best served when they select a particular combination of techniques, processes, and tools that fit their context and help them work in agreement with their chosen mindset. This combination can be considered the team's methodology.

There are a number of branded frameworks that fall under the broad banner of agile. These frameworks are collections of specific practices and ideas that have been proven useful in a specific context. These frameworks have some common characteristics:

- respect for people and the importance of creativity in delivering value,

- the importance of rapid delivery, feedback, and learning to ensure the product or service being produced meets real customer needs,

- collaboration and communication among the team members and the stakeholder community in order to build shared understanding, and

- break work into small slices of business value and deliver them incrementally and iteratively.

These frameworks include Scrum, Kanban, Extreme Programming, Adaptive Software Development, Lean Software Development, SAFe, LeSS, DAD, and many others.

It is important to understand that the context in which a framework worked at one time may not be the same as the context for a different initiative. There is no "one size fits all" in the agile mindset. The key to agility is to find what works in a particular context. Many teams find it helpful to combine techniques and practices from multiple frameworks to address the challenges of their context.

## 2.3     Applying the Agile Mindset

The ideas that inform the agile mindset were not new when they were synthesized into agile software development. As people practiced, spread, and refined these ideas, they found that the ideas can be applied to any domain that derives value from creative human work. These ideas have been used in marketing, running law and architecture firms, in consultancy organizations, in many different product development environments, in pharmaceutical product discovery, and a myriad of other domains.

All of these domains depend on human collaboration, skill, and knowledge to deliver value to the consumers of products. Business analysis shares these characteristics. Business analysis is a human-centric, exploratory, and creative endeavour, and analysis work results in changes to the way organizations run.

## 2.4     Agile Extension and the Agile Manifesto

The agile software development movement was founded on a document which encapsulates a philosophy of work, the Manifesto for Agile Software Development. This manifesto presents a set of values and principles which are the underpinning of the way of working embodied in agile software development.

The Manifesto for Agile Software Development (Agile Manifesto) was penned by a group of practitioners and methodologists who sought alternatives to the way software was developed at the time. A high percentage of software development initiatives were late, exceeded their planned budget, and didn't achieve their quality goals. The teams building software were stressed, unhappy, and dissatisfied with the working environment.

The Agile Manifesto states:

> *"We are uncovering better ways of developing*
> *software by doing it and helping others do it.*
> *Through this work we have come to value:*
>
> **Individuals and interactions** *over processes and tools*
> **Working software** *over comprehensive documentation*
> **Customer collaboration** *over contract negotiation*
> **Responding to change** *over following a plan*
>
> *That is, while there is value in the items on*
> *the right, we value the items on the left more."*

If we apply agile thinking to business analysis we can view these statements as guidelines for a philosophy of analysis.

These statements may be rooted in software development, but they can be related to agile business analysis in any context. Replacing "working software" with "working solution" expands our thinking and gives us guidance for an approach to analysis with an agile mindset.

### 1. We are uncovering better ways of delivering solutions by doing it and helping others do it.

This is the most important statement in the Agile Manifesto. It reinforces the practice based and empirical nature of the agile mindset. You learn what works by trying things out, not theorizing about what might work.

### 2. Individuals and interactions over processes and tools.

Business analysis is a human-centric activity. Business analysis practitioners start by understanding stakeholders' needs which requires them to work closely with stakeholders at every step of the value chain. Solutions frequently change the way people work, and agile business analysis practitioners make people the center of the work.

### 3. Working solutions over comprehensive documentation.

Agile business analysis practitioners focus on producing something, showing it to stakeholders, and eliciting immediate feedback to determine if they are on track to satisfying the need. Agile business analysis practitioners engage stakeholders in conversations in order to build and maintain shared understanding.

Documentation does provide value, but only when it's written to match its intended purpose. Agile business analysis practitioners produce documentation as they implement a change and use it to facilitate and support discussions with stakeholders.

### 4. Customer collaboration over contract negotiation.

Agile business analysis primarily focuses on satisfying needs. Business analysis practitioners learn to understand needs by showing increments of solutions to stakeholders and analyzing the feedback received. This ongoing collaboration with stakeholders facilitates new information about the need and constantly refines the understanding of the need until the need has been satisfied.

This ongoing collaboration with stakeholders also uncovers new needs based on customer demand, new competitors entering a market, government legislation that impacts the solution, or any other factor that may impact the solution.

### 5. Responding to change over following a plan.

Agile approaches do plan. In some contexts the plan is called the product roadmap. In an agile context, success is measured based on how well solutions satisfy the customer's needs and the value they derive from the solution. The ongoing learning and feedback that is central to the agile mindset allows for business analysis practitioners to continually refine their understanding of the need and make changes to the solution to ensure the solution satisfies the need.

It is the ability of agile business analysis practitioners to accurately respond to change that allows them to deliver value to their customers faster, with higher quality, and with the ability to rapidly change direction in response to changing conditions.

## 2.5    The Business Analysis Core Concept Model ™

The *Business Analysis Core Concept Model™ (BACCM™)* provides a conceptual framework for business analysis that is comprised of six terms that have a common meaning to all business analysis practitioners. Refer to *A Guide to the Business Analysis Body of Knowledge®* (*BABOK® Guide* ) version 3 for more information regarding the *Business Analysis Core Concept Model™*.

**Figure 2.5.1: The BACCM**

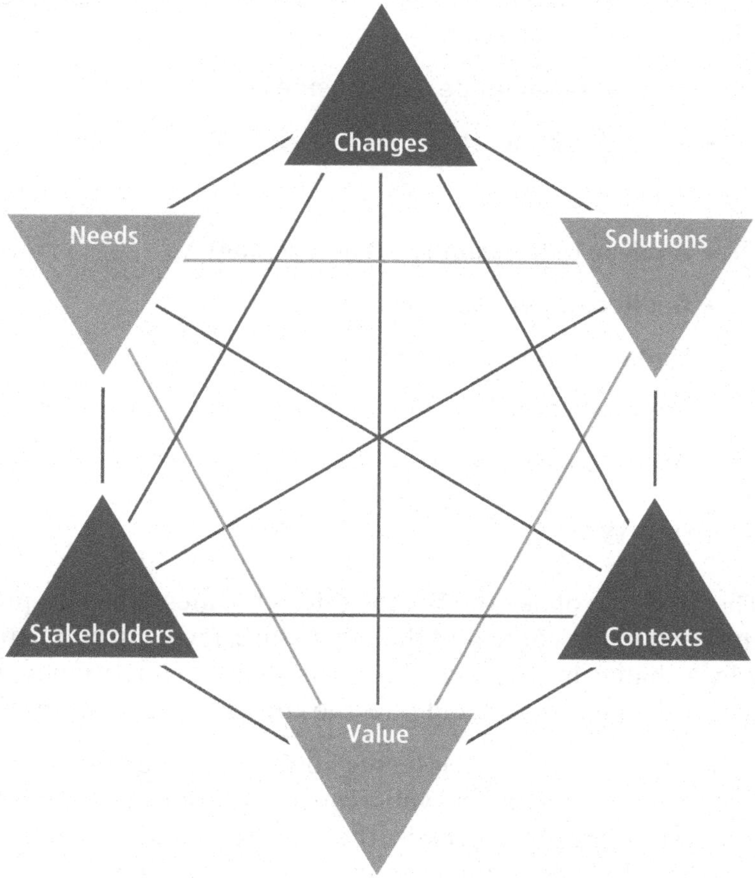

The six concepts of the model are:

- **Change**: The act of transformation in response to a need.

- **Need**: A problem or opportunity to be addressed.

- **Solution**: A specific way of satisfying one or more needs in a context.

- **Stakeholder**: A group or individual with a relationship to the change, the need, or the solution.

- **Value**: The worth, importance, or usefulness of something to a stakeholder within a context.

- **Context**: The circumstances that influence, are influenced by, and provide understanding of the change.

These concepts are common to all business analysis practitioners, and they can apply to any domain and any level in the organization. They provide a universal language to describe how to approach business analysis with an agile mindset.

## 2.6 Principles of Agile Business Analysis

The Agile Manifesto provides a set of values that form the foundation of the agile mindset. The *BABOK® Guide* presents the *Business Analysis Core Concept Model™* which provides a set of core concepts and common language to describe business analysis. The *Agile Extension to the BABOK® Guide* describes seven principles for agile business analysis.

The principles that guide agile business analysis are:

- See the Whole

- Think as a Customer

- Analyze to Determine What is Valuable

- Get Real Using Examples

- Understand What is Doable

- Stimulate Collaboration and Continuous Improvement

- Avoid Waste

### 2.6.1 See the Whole

The principle of See the Whole guides business analysis practitioners to analyze the need in the context of the big picture, focusing on the business context and why a change is necessary. Business analysis practitioners examine the context in which the need exists and how the context influences the solution.

Agile business analysis assesses how the solution delivers value when satisfying stakeholders' needs. The value for the solution is created through gaining an understanding of the context, the solution, and the stakeholders. The ideas behind See the Whole are influenced by systems thinking.

### 2.6.2 Think as a Customer

The principle of Think as a Customer guides business analysis practitioners in ensuring solutions incorporate the voice of the customer through a clear understanding of the expected user experience.

A customer can be any stakeholder that interacts with the solution. Business analysis practitioners generally start with a high-level view of customer needs and progressively decompose these viewpoints into an increasingly detailed understanding of the needs the solution must satisfy. Agile approaches incorporate feedback loops to continuously validate this learning. As solution delivery progresses, both the customer's and the organization's understanding of the needs evolve. Feedback and learning is central to ensuring these changes are incorporated into future iterations of the solution.

### 2.6.3      Analyze to Determine What is Valuable

The principle of Analyze to Determine What is Valuable guides business analysis practitioners to continuously assess and prioritize work to be done in order to maximize the value being delivered at any point in time.

Determining what is valuable involves understanding the purpose of requirements and ensuring solution options and solution components continue to support the desired outcome. This includes avoiding waste by maximizing the amount of work not done and delivering valuable solutions early and continuously.

### 2.6.4      Get Real Using Examples

The principle of Get Real Using Examples guides business analysis practitioners in building a shared understanding of the need and how the solution will satisfy that need.

These examples can be used to iteratively develop and elaborate analysis models to explore multiple dimensions (for example, user role, user actions, data, and business rules) of a need. This practice continuously engages stakeholders and supports a shared understanding of needs.

The level of abstraction of examples and models varies depending on the audience and the outcome being sought. For example, when planning the product, examples or models can be used to set context and identify scope. These models are more abstract and provide a broad perspective of the need. When delivering the product, the examples or models can be progressively elaborated to identify specific details of the need and the solution.

Examples can also be used to derive acceptance criteria, help design the solution, and provide a foundation for testing the solution.

### 2.6.5      Understand What is Doable

The principle of Understand What is Doable guides business analysis practitioners to understand how to deliver a solution within given constraints. Constraints can include the capabilities of the technology used to deliver the solution, the skills of the team, and the time in which you have to deliver a valuable solution.

Understanding what is doable involves continually analyzing the need and the solutions that can satisfy that need within the known constraints. It also involves considering measures such as team capacity and velocity trends to maintain reasonable expectations on an ongoing basis.

### 2.6.6 Stimulate Collaboration and Continuous Improvement

The principle of Stimulate Collaboration and Continuous Improvement guides business analysis practitioners in creating and contributing to an environment where all stakeholders contribute value on an ongoing basis.

Agile approaches emphasize the usefulness of continual collaboration between those with a need and those who are delivering a solution to meet that need.

A key aspect of the agile mindset is continuous improvement. Business analysis practitioners seek to continually improve the solution as well as the processes used to deliver the solution. Continuous structured and unstructured feedback allows business analysis practitioners to adapt the solution and its processes in order to increase the value being delivered.

Retrospectives are also used to examine processes and solutions, and identify opportunities for improvement. Healthy, collaborative teams have the trust and safety necessary to transparently identify opportunities for improvement and implement them.

### 2.6.7 Avoid Waste

The principle of Avoid Waste guides business analysis practitioners in identifying which activities add value and which activities do not add value. Agile business analysis seeks to understand the need and to deliver a solution that satisfies that need. Any activity that does not contribute directly to this goal is waste.

Waste can be divided into two sets of activities:

- those that have value but do not directly contribute to satisfying the need, and

- those activities that do not add value at all.

The aim is to completely remove those activities that do not add value, and minimize those activities that do not directly contribute to satisfying the need.

When avoiding waste, agile business analysis practitioners

- avoid producing documentation before it is needed, and when documentation is needed do just enough,

- ensure commitments are met and there are no incomplete work items that adversely impact downstream activities,

- avoid rework by making commitments at the last responsible moment,

- try to elicit, analyze, specify, and validate requirements with the same models,

- make analysis models as simple as possible to meet their intended purpose,

- ensure clear and effective communication, and

- pay continuous attention to technical excellence and accuracy. Quality defects (such as unclear requirements) result in rework and are waste.

## 2.7 The Business Analysis Core Concept Model™ and the Principles of Agile Business Analysis

The *Business Analysis Core Concept Model™* (*BACCM™*) provides set of core concepts and common language for business analysis. The seven principles of agile business analysis provide guidance on applying the agile mind set to business analysis activities.

The principles of agile business analysis can be mapped to the core concepts as listed below.

**Table 2.7.1: The BACCM and Principles of Agile Business Analysis**

| Core Concept | BACCM™ Definition | Principle of Agile Business Analysis |
|---|---|---|
| Change | The act of transformation in response to a need | Change is central to all principles of agile business analysis. |
| Need | A problem or opportunity to be addressed. | Get Real Using Examples. |
| Solution | A specific way of satisfying one or more needs in a context. | Simulate Collaboration and Continuous Improvements. |
| Stakeholder | A group or individual with a relationship to the change, the need, or the solution. | Think as a Customer. |

| Core Concept | BACCM™ Definition | Principle of Agile Business Analysis |
|---|---|---|
| Value | The worth, importance, or usefulness of something to a stakeholder within a context. | Get Real Using Examples and Avoid Waste. |
| Context | The circumstances that influence, are influenced by, and provide understanding of the change. | See the Whole. |

# Analysis at Multiple Horizons

A planning horizon represents a view of work within an organization with a level of granularity appropriate to the planning time frame and the nature of the feedback loops. The *Agile Extension* defines three horizons: Strategy, Initiative, and Delivery. This framework provides a model to describe agile business analysis. Individual practitioners and organizations may employ different terms, levels of granularity, and time frames based on the context of the organization and the work being done.

In constant and rapidly changing environments, organizations are required to be able to sense and respond to local opportunities and problems without the need to involve the whole organization, while also looking forward at emerging threats and opportunities. These planning horizons provide a framework for the shift in focus that occurs when moving between understanding the long-term strategic needs of the organization and the immediate needs of a customer.

Depending on the size of the organization, multiple business analysis practitioners may be independently focusing on individual horizons and continuously communicating with each other, or a single business analysis practitioner may focus on more than one horizon. Constant communication and collaboration across all horizons is essential to allow for rapid feedback and learning which supports effective decision making across the organization.

## 3.1      Overview of the Three Horizons

### 3.1.1      The Strategy Horizon

The Strategy Horizon refers to the decisions that impact the entire organization. Business analysis practitioners operating at this horizon support decisions about strategy and the allocation of available resources in support of that strategy.

Decisions made at the Strategy Horizon identify the products, services, and initiatives to which the organization allocates resources.

Business analysis practitioners working at the Strategy Horizon identify short-term goals, initiatives, and risks that align to organizational strategy, and articulate the problems that must be understood in order to make strategic decisions.

The time horizon of the Strategy Horizon may be as short as three months to as long as multiple years ahead. This time frame continually shifts and moves forward, creating what can be considered a rolling time frame.

Business analysis practitioners working at the Strategy Horizon constantly consider what can be done to add value and how to learn valuable lessons quickly.

For more details regarding the Strategy Horizon, see 4. Strategy Horizon.

### 3.1.2      The Initiative Horizon

The Initiative Horizon refers to decisions that impact a particular goal, initiative, or team. Business analysis practitioners operating at this horizon support initiative based decisions about how to create value with the resources available, as well as better understanding the needs of the stakeholders and the options available.

At the Initiative Horizon, business analysis practitioners support decisions that are acted on in a shorter time period than at the Strategy Horizon and over a longer period of time than at the Delivery Horizon. Feedback and learning at the Initiative Horizon supports the analysis being done at both the Strategy Horizon and the Delivery Horizon.

Agile business analysis at the Initiative Horizon may support decision makers in a single team or in multiple teams. Each team may work independently or they may be highly interdependent, leading to a need to understand complex dependencies between teams.

For more details regarding the Initiative Horizon, see 5. Initiative Horizon.

### 3.1.3      The Delivery Horizon

The Delivery Horizon refers to decisions made regarding the delivery of the solution. Business analysis practitioners operating at this horizon work with the delivery team to understand how to best break down work, how to deliver and test the value the team is creating, and how to learn quickly from the work the team is doing.

The team working at the Delivery Horizon works on prioritized work from the backlog and turns it into a valuable product or service that meets the identified outcome or goal of the solution.

At the Delivery Horizon, business analysis practitioners support decisions that are acted on in a shorter time period than at the Initiative Horizon and impact the solution currently being developed. Business analysis practitioners work with a variety of stakeholders including decision makers and customers to deliver value directly to the customer.

For more details regarding the Delivery Horizon, see 6. Delivery Horizon.

## 3.2      Agility at Each Horizon

The same agile mindset, the same agile principles, and even many of the same agile business analysis practices apply at each horizon. However, different people may be involved in the analysis performed at each horizon, and the practices and techniques may apply in different ways. Appendix B: Mapping BABOK Guide Tasks to Horizons provides an overview of how each of the Tasks from the *BABOK® Guide* can be applied at each horizon. The individual chapters on each horizon also discuss the specific practices and techniques that are commonly used.

Agile business analysis involves continuous collaboration, feedback, and learning for all stakeholders across all horizons. This ongoing collaboration provides more current and accurate information to decision makers to help them make better decisions and achieve better outcomes.

The following diagram illustrates the interactivity between the three horizons.

**Figure 3.2.1: Three Planning Horizon**

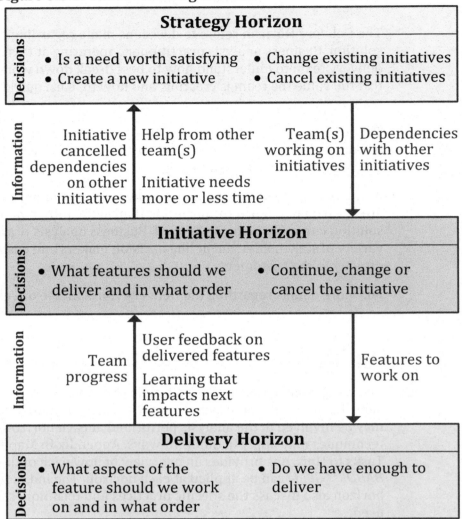

## 3.3 Predictive, Iterative, and Adaptive Planning

There are many ways in which business analysis practitioners plan. At the highest level, there are three most commonly used approaches to planning: predictive, iterative, and adaptive.

This chapter discusses these three planning approaches in their basic and root forms. Business analysis practitioners and the organizations in which they work may employ any combination of these planning approaches that suits their context.

### 3.3.1 Predictive Planning

Predictive planning involves performing detailed analysis and planning and then acting on that planning. An economic driver for predictive planning is the "cost of change" curve. It suggests that the later a mistake is found, the more it will cost to fix it. This in turn suggests that it is cheaper to spend more time analyzing information early on, so as to provide the fewest possible misunderstandings, gaps, and defects as possible before more work is done.

**Figure 3.3.1: Cost of Change Curve**

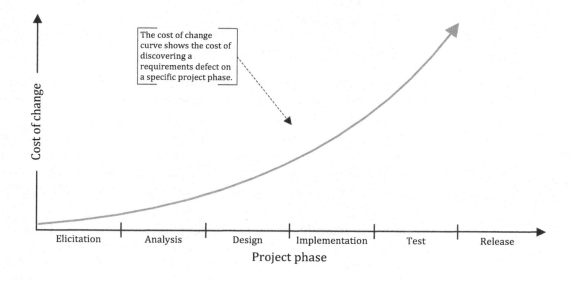

Predictive planning attempts to predict scope and risk at the beginning of a project. The planning horizon of predictive planning is the duration of the project, and project managers will therefore construct a detailed plan for the entire duration of the project. Deviations from the plan are seen as risks and a considerable body of practice exists for getting a deviant project "back on track". Feedback and learning can be suppressed in favour of maintaining the original plan.

A well prepared planner may identify potential risks and develop contingency plans based on good analysis. The challenge is that the cost of change can be high if a potential issue or opportunity means changing a substantial amount of detail as well. An unforeseen event can disrupt the plan, or worse, an opportunity cannot be accommodated because the work involved in changing the plan makes it impractical.

### 3.3.2    Iterative Planning

Iterative planning is an approach that is frequently used when long-term planning is rendered ineffective by rapid change and great uncertainty: the next step in the plan is based on the latest learning.

This suggests that each hypothesis should be tested before planning what to do next, since the hypothesis might be right, wrong, or partially right. In this situation, stakeholders and subject matter experts are learning what they need at the same time as planning is occurring. This suggests that plans are only viable for the immediate future, potentially the next one to four weeks.

Business analysis practitioners identify opportunities and threats as they emerge through the constant testing of assumptions. They are able to react to potential risks because the plans are resilient and constantly evolving.

In a rapidly changing, large, or complex context, not all information is immediately apparent or fully understood. Business analysis practitioners might find they have insufficient time to analyze an idea that impacts many parts of the solution, or they may find that they are doing a lot of rework as they discover new information or needs.

### 3.3.3     Adaptive Planning

Adaptive planning requires both long- and short-term planning. Long-term plans are subject to change though and are easy to change. Short-term plans take into account and inform the long-term plans of the organization.

This comes at a cost. It means that the organization is constantly both planning and analyzing. This creates confusion, mistakes, and wasted effort if there is a lack of transparency, trust, and collaboration. Adaptive planning creates a context that supports an agile mindset and the adoption of agile approaches to business analysis.

Adaptive planning is central to agile business analysis. Organizations produce both long-term and short-term plans, but it is not planning in a linear way. Adaptive planning (sometimes referred to as rolling wave planning) treats each plan as a hypothesis to be proven. Feedback and lessons learned are used to adjust the plan in real time. Newly discovered information may change the hypotheses on which the plan is based and cause a change in the plan. If not, business analysis practitioners continue to uncover better ways to achieve the plan as they execute it.

Adaptive planning is an effective approach when there is value in fast feedback and learning, and also in long-term planning. Higher level planning horizons (strategy and initiative), are longer and information more abstract than the lower planning horizons (initiative and delivery). Resistance to change is lessened because there is less detail to change.

## 3.3.4    Summary of Planning Approaches

### Table 3.3.1: Summary of Planning Approaches

| Approach | Economic Assumption | Planning Horizon | Issues and benefits |
|---|---|---|---|
| Adaptive | Cost of change increases as project progresses. Opportunity cost is high if feedback and learning are suppressed. Learning is facilitated by ongoing analysis and feedback. Implementation is continuous and creates learning for future work. | Plan is continuous and nested (or fractal) where strategic planning provides vision and scope to initiatives, while information gathered as work is delivered informs strategic thinking. | Significant complexity updating and adapting plans, which requires continuous collaboration and feedback. Appears inefficient because of the effort required to adapt plans as feedback and learning are generated. Cost of change is reduced because the organization can rapidly "sense and respond to" new information, while also keeping a focus on the longer term goals of the organization. |
| Iterative | Cost of change is flat and does not increase as project progresses. High opportunity cost if feedback and learning are suppressed. Learning is best facilitated by quickly building the systems and soliciting feedback. | Plan is a series of short-term, detailed horizons. A plan is created only for the current horizon (iteration) and takes advantage of the latest feedback and learning. | Highly responsive to learning. Very efficient as there is no plan to maintain. Does not scale well and can appear ad-hoc because teams are encouraged to see beyond the horizon visible to them. Lack of focus on a longer range objective can result in planning becoming ad-hoc and random. |
| Predictive | Cost of change grows exponentially. Low opportunity cost with suppressed learning because project scope can be defined early. Learning is best facilitated by upfront analysis. | Plan consists of a single long-term, detailed horizon generally spanning the duration of the project. A detailed plan is constructed at the beginning of the project and all work is measured in terms of conformance to the plan. | Slow to respond to learning and may even suppress learning. Well understood by any organization. Efficiency is created by certainty in executing existing plans. |

# 4 Strategy Horizon

## 4.1 Purpose

The purpose of analysis at the Strategy Horizon is to inform decisions regarding the organization's business goals.

## 4.2 Description

Value is created at the Strategy Horizon through understanding and achieving the business' goals. Business goals change; consumer tastes change; competitors create disruptive technology; regulations change. At the Strategy Horizon, the priority of business goals are continually reassessed and emerging opportunities evaluated. Agile business analysis enables organizations to rapidly and effectively adapt the organization's business goals and quickly redeploy the organization's available resources.

Organizations that are agile embrace change. They redeploy their resources as fast as they learn what the evolving business goals are. At the Strategy Horizon, the information that informs these decisions is frequently overwhelming, obscure, uncertain, and even contradictory. In rapidly changing contexts, there is a risk that strategic decisions may be made on outdated data. Even if clear, understandable information is available, effectively communicating this information is challenging. The lack of effective communication to stakeholders creates the risk that decisions may be made on the wrong information, even though dependable information exists within the organization. Agile business analysis responds to these challenges by enabling quick and effective decision making in complex and rapidly changing contexts.

While the practices and techniques used at the Strategy Horizon may differ from those employed at the Initiative and Delivery Horizons, the principles, mindset, and capabilities needed for agile business analysis are consistent throughout all three Horizons.

## 4.3 Elements

### 4.3.1 Observe Change Across a Broad Horizon

The value of agile business analysis at the Strategic Horizon is founded in the broad scope of the analysis and the ability to communicate information across the organization – both to senior decision makers and to those operating within different initiatives within the organization.

Agile business analysis is aware of the need for timeliness of observations. It ensures that observations of change are acted upon sufficiently quickly to make them relevant to the decision process.

#### .1 Scope of Analysis

Agile business analysis has a broad scope at the Strategic Horizon. Its scope of analysis is beyond the individual initiative and involves analyzing and communicating information learned from the organizational context. At the Strategic Horizon, agile business analysis involves making sense of changes across the following areas:

- **Changes to customer expectations**: teams working on initiatives notice changes in customer expectations resulting from new product introductions and the resulting social and economic changes. There are also changes to customer expectations that are not visible to these teams. At the Strategy Horizon, the scope of analysis extends beyond individual initiatives and involves analyzing and communicating information received through customer research and analytics, as well as research into emerging customer trends.

- **Changes to the outside environment**: organizations exist within an organizational context where competitors are constantly innovating, economic and social conditions are changing, and new technologies are emerging at a rapid rate. Business analysis practitioners constantly monitor and evaluate these changes, forming new hypotheses and changing old assumptions.

- **Changes within the organization**: organizations constantly change. As a result, organizations must constantly redirect resources and potentially set new goals. Agile business analysis provides timely, useful information to those making decisions based on internal changes.

- **Learning from the front line**: teams operating at the Initiative and Delivery Horizons are constantly making changes and discoveries. Some of this information has an impact on the goals and resource allocation beyond the initiative. A major economic driver for agile adoption is the ability to quickly learn which initiatives to stop funding because they either have delivered their promised value or have not realized their potential value, or on which initiatives to increase resources because they have opened new strategic opportunities. At the Strategy Horizon, business analysis practitioners synthesize and analyze information from multiple initiatives in order to inform decisions that impact the organization's business goals and priorities.

- **Threats and opportunities**: with constant change occurring within and beyond the organization, new threats and opportunities appear (and fade) constantly.
  Agile business analysis practitioners continually analyze threats and opportunities that enable the organization to

  - start a new initiative to counter a threat or exploit an opportunity,

  - change the resourcing, scope, or success criteria for existing initiatives in response to changing circumstances, and

  - cancel an existing initiative that has become less relevant or less likely to succeed.

At the Strategy Horizon, the focus of business analysis is on the discovery and analysis of evolving threats and opportunities. Successful outcomes depend on decisions being made quickly and correctly on changes as they occur.

## 4.3.2  Level of Detail

At the Strategy Horizon, business analysis practitioners are required to understand the organizational goals and how they map to the goals of individual initiatives. Analysis at the Strategy Horizon generally stops before getting into the details of specific initiatives. Business analysis practitioners working within each initiative are generally better placed to analyze information, collaborate with stakeholders, and inform good decision making for the initiative.

At the Strategy Horizon, business analysis practitioners identify a potential need and then provide enough detail to the team working at the Initiative Horizon for them to understand the need and develop potential solutions and features.

The detailed analysis of the solution is done at the Initiative and Delivery Horizons. At the Strategy Horizon, business analysis practitioners focus on risks, changing circumstances, and new needs that might change the prioritization of decisions made by the organization as multiple initiatives progress.

Due to the great need for collaboration, feedback, and learning between the Strategy, Initiative, and Delivery Horizons, there is no clean line where the responsibility for analysis is handed over from one business analysis practitioner to another.

### 4.3.3     Reducing Complexity to Support Decision Making

At the Strategy Horizon, agile business analysis involves breaking down systems and ideas into small parts to understand each component sufficiently to either create a new solution, solve a specific problem, or modify an existing solution.

The systems being analyzed (for example, the performance of individual initiatives, the actions of competitors, and the changing inputs to strategy) are unstable and understanding is always incomplete. Business analysis practitioners use tools such as models to reduce the complexity of large volumes of confusing data, and enable decision makers to have sufficient information to make a defensible and testable decision.

## 4.4     Time Frames

The Strategic Horizon involves looking further into the future than the Initiative and Delivery Horizons. While some analysis does happen in real time, much of it focuses on speculating on what might happen in the future. How far the organization looks ahead depends on the organization and the context in which it is operating. Business analysis practitioners may look as short as three months, to as long as multiple years ahead. This time frame continually shifts and moves forward, creating what can be considered a rolling time frame.

When looking into the distant future business analysis practitioners consider broad analysis and uncertain data. Analysis is likely to be at a higher level and more abstract than when looking at the immediate future. The further business analysis practitioners look into the future, the more plans and models become aspirational and a hypothesis to be tested, rather than facts. When considering the distant future, the business analysis practitioner constantly asks the question "as an organization, what do we need to learn to either prove or disprove our long-term hypothesis?"

At the Strategy Horizon, business analysis practitioners continually switch their analysis from understanding the micro-details of a potential change to understanding the broader view of the impact of the change and the opportunities it might present to the organization as a whole.

## 4.5     Feedback and Learning

Decision makers frequently delay launching initiatives until the information they have provides them with confidence that the initiative will be successful. These decisions to delay are made because decision makers lack the ability to learn quickly and make timely strategic decisions.

At the Strategy Horizon, agile business analysis provides just enough information to decide whether to begin a new initiative. Specifically, this means answering the questions:

- Is there a need to satisfy?

- Is the need aligned with the organization's strategic objectives?

- Is it worth satisfying that need?

- Do we believe we have the right team to provide a good enough solution?

- Are we able to measure the success of the initiative?

Once the decision to start a new initiative is made, further analysis is done at the Initiative Horizon.

Communications between Horizons is a continuous process of feedback and learning. Analysis done at the Strategy Horizon provides useful information to teams at the Initiative and Delivery Horizons. Learning is created at both the Initiative and Delivery Horizons that enables effective decision making at the Strategy Horizon.

Continuous and timely feedback loops enable rapid decision making. The constant flow of information from multiple initiatives to the decision makers at the Strategy Horizon facilitates the making of timely strategic decisions.

At the Strategy Horizon, business analysis practitioners continuously analyze and communicate information that is available at the Initiative Horizon. Business analysis practitioners operating at the Strategy Horizon collaborate closely with the business analysis practitioners operating at the Initiative Horizon.

Agile business analysis at the Strategy Horizon involves analyzing large amounts of changing data with complex relationships. This generally involves multiple business analysis practitioners conducting analysis in different areas and multiple decision makers from different domains making independent decisions. For example, an accountant might be looking at changes to cash flows while a marketing manager is looking at changes in customer behaviour. Each independent decision may have an impact on the outcome of other decisions made elsewhere in the organization. Business analysis practitioners play a central role in facilitating the continuous feedback and learning between stakeholders within the Strategy Horizon.

## 4.6 Applying the Principles of Agile Business Analysis

### 4.6.1 See the Whole

At the Strategy Horizon, the agile principle of See the Whole is applied when business analysis practitioners work with decision makers in order to make effective decisions. Decisions at the Strategy Horizon incorporate a holistic view of the context in which the organization exists (the market, the political climate and many other factors). Decisions are also based on a realistic understanding of the current capabilities, strengths and challenges of the organization itself.

Agile business analysis facilitates a holistic understanding of the organization and its environment through constant analysis and evaluation, creating rapid feedback cycles and learning throughout the organization. It also facilitates a holistic understanding through constant, deep collaboration between business analysis practitioners and stakeholders throughout the organization.

### 4.6.2     Think as a Customer

At the Strategy Horizon, the agile principle of Think as a Customer is applied when business analysis practitioners maintain a strategic focus on customer value.

Thinking as a customer provides a clear focus on customer value and helps the organization to set goals and align work across the organization. Without customer focus, teams focused on the Initiative Horizon might create individual customer experiences that would be good as isolated experiences but create an inconsistent or sub-optimal experience when combined into an ongoing customer journey.

Agile business analysis facilitates a customer focus by communicating learning between teams and by enabling decision makers to align the limited resources of the organization to most effectively focus on the greatest overall customer value.

### 4.6.3     Analyze to Determine What is Valuable

At the Strategy Horizon, the agile principle of Analyze to Determine What is Valuable is applied when identifying the strategic needs to be met.

Business analysis practitioners help decision makers better allocate resources in the pursuit of the organization's goals. This ensures that work done across the organization creates the most value possible for the effort expended.

In a rapidly changing environment, goals and plans are stable. New learning must be analyzed quickly and effectively on an ongoing basis and decisions must be made on recent, potentially uncertain data. Agile business analysis helps decision makers at the Strategy Horizon understand what is truly valuable as the organizational context evolves.

### 4.6.4     Get Real Using Examples

At the Strategy Horizon, the agile principle of Get Real Using Examples is applied when communicating current evidence based information to decision makers.

Effective planning is based on information that is relevant, easy to understand, and up to date. In a context of continuous change, there is a risk of making poorly informed decisions because projections or assumptions are out of date. There is also a risk that decision makers may make important decisions based on opinions or misunderstood evidence. Business analysis practitioners constantly identify new changes that impact planning assumptions and articulate the potential impact of those changes.

Agile business analysis is based on real evidence and real examples that occur in real time. This supports evidence-based decisions in rapidly changing and uncertain environments. A good example of this is the decision to start a new initiative. This decision should be based on effective analysis of the most current and reliable information available. Business analysis practitioners communicate the goals of the initiative, what is known, and which untested hypotheses they believe to be true. This allows the initiative team to better understand what can be achieved and when the initiative should be cancelled or re-scoped based on new information.

## 4.6.5 Understand What is Doable

At the Strategy Horizon, the agile principle of Understand What is Doable is applied when making strategic decisions regarding the organization's resources and the strategic needs the organization wishes to satisfy.

Planning at the Strategy Horizon is challenging. There are often numerous threats and opportunities to choose from, and there are impediments to redeploying the organization's resources in response to the latest information. The sheer volume of information that must be digested by decision makers means that deciding what to act on is a major challenge.

Business analysis practitioners continuously interpret the significance of new information in a way that decision makers can make effective decisions without being distracted by important seeming, but ultimately irrelevant, information. When this is done, decision makers can quickly decide what should be done next to add customer value, outperform competitors, or respond to emerging threats.

## 4.6.6 Stimulate Collaboration and Continuous Improvement

At the Strategy Horizon, the agile principle of Stimulate Collaboration and Continuous Improvement is applied to the agile organization's culture as a means of developing and supporting high-performing teams.

Collaboration and continuous improvement are core components of any high-performing team. It becomes increasingly difficult to collaborate and innovate as the size and number of teams increases in an organization. It is important the organization develop effective channels that allow teams that interact with customers to respond quickly, while sharing and benefiting from the learning that is happening across the rest of the organization.

At the Strategy Horizon, business analysis practitioners add value by facilitating the transfer of relevant knowledge between teams. This speeds the collaboration and continuous improvement because the teams learn quickly from each other and are not impeded by having to rely on a central authority to determine what they should know and what they should share.

## 4.6.7 Avoid Waste

At the Strategy Horizon, the agile principle of Avoid Waste is applied when business analysis practitioners ensure decisions are made on current and accurate information, and when the entire organization has a shared understanding of the organization's goals and priorities.

At the Strategy Horizon, waste is created when:

- decisions are based on bad information,

- initiatives deliver outcomes that are not aligned with each other, duplicate each other, or undermine the work done by other initiatives, and

- resources continue to be allocated to an initiative that no longer delivers value.

At the Strategy Horizon, business analysis practitioners reduce waste by providing the right information to

- teams at the Initiative Horizon about what is happening in the rest of the organization so they can make more effective local decisions,

- decision makers to support decisions about which initiatives should be initiated or cancelled, and

- organizational leaders regarding which initiatives will benefit most from the allocation of available resources.

# 4.7 Techniques

## 4.7.1 Agile Extension Techniques

- **Minimal Viable Product**: used to prioritize the allocation of resources and to increase the speed of organizational learning.

- **Planning Workshop**: used to plan the allocation or resources across multiple initiatives and to provide a shared understanding of the purpose of a new initiative.

- **Portfolio Kanban**: used to provide real time visibility of the progress of initiatives across the portfolio. May also be used in conjunction with Balanced Scorecards, Value Stream Maps and other approaches to optimize the allocation of resources across initiatives.

- **Product Roadmap**: used to communicate the expected future direction of the product and to improve collaboration among teams in different initiatives. Also used to support decision making and prioritization.

- **Purpose Alignment Model**: used to prioritize potential initiatives, understand the optimum resourcing mix on initiatives and to understand the overall focus of initiatives across the organization.

- **Real Options**: used to understand the appropriate time for making decisions.

- **Relative Estimating**: used to quickly understand the relative value and resource requirements of potential initiatives across the portfolio.

- **Value Stream Mapping**: used to understand the creation of value across the whole customer experience to prioritize, plan and integrate the creation of value and reduction of waste between initiatives across the portfolio.

- **Visioning**: used to understand decision options and clarify the organization's vision. Also used to identify the purpose and focus for a new initiative.

## 4.7.2      BABOK® Guide Techniques

- **Backlog Management**: used to track initiatives across the portfolio of work and also to understand critical risks, integration needs, and dependencies between initiatives.

- **Balanced Scorecard**: used to track value and measure progress across initiatives through continuous reporting and feedback across the core focus areas in the organization.

- **Benchmarking and Market Analysis**: used to provide input into decisions made in real time and to provide useful information to teams across the organization to support decision making and collaboration.

- **Business Capability Analysis**: used to support decision making and to provide input to teams making decisions that impact multiple initiatives.

- **Business Cases**: used to consider alternative approaches to solving strategic problems and to launch new initiatives.

- **Business Model Canvas**: used to consider multiple options when launching initiatives and to help scope the work of a new initiative. Also used to look at how value is created, captured, and delivered to stakeholders across the organization to allow decisions to made quickly at a strategic level, and to understand the impact of changes to both the organization and its environment.

- **Metrics and Key Performance Indicators (KPIs)**: used to communicate priorities and measure delivery across the organization. Also used to communicate what the organization defines as necessary to create value.

- **Organizational Modelling**: used to prioritize initiatives and understand the available resources that can be used in initiatives. Also used to ensure that business value is created across the organization rather than seeing individual initiatives create products and services that cannot be delivered effectively by the wider organization.

- **Risk Analysis and Management**: used to inform decisions in real time. Also used to prioritize new initiatives and to understand the need for changing priorities based on changing circumstances beyond the horizon of a single initiative.

- **Stakeholder List, Map, or Personas**: used to identify the people who need to be involved in decisions.

- **SWOT Analysis**: used to understand the context in which decisions will be made and to prioritize new initiatives.

- **Vendor Assessment**: used to understand the capabilities possessed by potential partners and vendors. Also used to understand the capabilities and available resources that vendors can provide to initiatives across the portfolio of work.

# 5 Initiative Horizon

## 5.1 Purpose

The purpose of analysis at the Initiative Horizon is to inform decisions regarding solution options, features, priorities, and lifespan.

## 5.2 Description

Analysis performed at the Initiative Horizon is concerned with the decisions surrounding defining and delivering a solution that satisfies a need identified at the Strategy Horizon. The goal of this analysis is to deliver a solution in a way that minimizes output and maximizes outcome. The information that supports this goal include the answers to the following questions:

- What solution options satisfy the need?

- Which solution option appears to provide the maximum outcome with the minimum output and fits within the given constraints?

- What are the solution components as described by features of the preferred solution option?

- What features should be delivered now, next, and in the future?

- Has enough value been delivered to satisfy the need?

- Based on ongoing feedback and learning, should the solution continue, change, or be cancelled?

Decisions made at the Initiative Horizon align with the decisions made at the Strategy Horizon. The Strategy Horizon informs decisions at the Initiative Horizon through the continuous communication of

- the shared understanding of the need to be satisfied,

- why the need exists, and

- the determination that the need is worth satisfying, given the organization's current understanding of benefits, risks, and constraints.

The Initiative Horizon is largely about the amount and type of analysis required to be done in order to support a series of decisions. These decisions start with defining the need being satisfied and conclude with identifying the aspects of the solution that will satisfy that need.

At the Initiative Horizon, business analysis practitioners use feedback from the Strategy and Delivery Horizons to determine if the solution is producing the anticipated outcome. Analysis of that feedback results in a decision to continue, change, or cancel the current solution.

# 5.3 Elements

## 5.3.1 Size of Items

Analysis performed at the Initiative Horizon is concerned with the many activities involved in an initiative in order to accomplish a specific outcome. Most solutions are complex enough that there are multiple solution options that can all deliver the same outcome, and each solution has multiple solution components. In an agile context these solution components are referred to as features.

## 5.3.2 Identifying Solution Options

At the Initiative Horizon, business analysis practitioners identify solution options worth considering for implementation. Multiple solution options allow the agile team to analyze each option to determine whether each option is viable or not.

In order to make this decision, the team requires a shared understanding of the need to be satisfied and the desired outcome. That shared understanding includes clear and measurable objectives. These objectives can be used to do an initial assessment of solution options to determine if they are viable and will provide sufficient progress toward the outcome.

When assessing solution options, business analysis practitioners consider:

- the shared understanding of the need to satisfy,

- any assumptions surrounding what will make a viable solution,

- the risks that satisfying the need will introduce,

- a very broad description of every solution option, and

- the constraints that may make some solution options nonviable.

Part of the process of generating solution options includes the discovery of previously unknown information which informs decisions around the viability of solution options.

### 5.3.3    Recommending Solution Options

At the Initiative Horizon, business analysis practitioners recommend the solution options based on which solution option provides the maximum outcome with the minimum output and fits within identified constraints. The business leader or decision maker who is responsible for the solution generally makes the decision to proceed with the recommended solution option or not.

In order to accurately assess different solution options, the information being analyzed is at the same level of precision for each solution option under consideration. The level of precision of the information should be appropriate to the decision being made and provide just enough information to make an informed and accurate decision.

When recommending solution options, business analysis practitioners:

- validate any made assumptions when identifying solution options,

- identify methods of assessing the implementation practicality,

- consider information about the people, processes, tools, organizations, systems, vendors, and other external entities that are impacted by the solution to identify potential conflicts or risks,

- assess the solution's projected impact on the identified need, and

- estimate the cost of each solution option in terms of time, money, or any other resource relevant for the team.

Experimentation can be a useful process to engage in when selecting a solution option. When recommending a solution option, the goal of experimentation is to discover just enough information to enable the selection of an option.

### 5.3.4    Identifying Solution Components

Solutions are comprised of multiple solution components. At the Initiative Horizon, business analysis practitioners collaborate with stakeholders to identify different possible aspects and parts of the solution that will provide the desired outcome. Some agile contexts refer to solution components as features. The decision maker who is responsible for the solution generally makes the decision to proceed with the identified solution components or not.

Each identified component is evaluated in the context of the desired outcome, costs, impacts, and constraints. The information being analyzed is at the same moderate level of precision for each solution option under consideration and provides just enough information to make an informed and accurate decision. This creates a list of components which could be used to develop the selected solution option. Many agile contexts consider this list to be the backlog.

Identifying solution components is an ongoing iterative process, with solution components being continually refined as more information is discovered and a greater understanding of the need and solution option is gained. New items may be added to the list and others removed as the understanding of the value of each individual solution component becomes apparent.

### 5.3.5 Prioritizing Solution Components

Once the potential solution components are identified, business analysis practitioners prioritize and sequence the components. In some agile contexts this process is referred to as refining the backlog. The decision maker who is responsible for the solution generally makes the decision on the priorities and sequencing of solution components.

Business analysis practitioners assess the priority and sequence of solution components based on:

- the impact that each solution component has on the overall outcome,
- the cost (either actual or in terms of team capacity) in implementing the solution component,
- the current state of the initiative,
- feedback from stakeholders,
- current performance toward the desired outcome, and
- current understanding of the constraints and risks.

The prioritization and sequencing of solution components occurs multiple times throughout the course of an initiative. When new information is discovered that leads to a change to solution components, priority and sequence are reassessed to ensure alignment with the new information. The priority and sequence of solution components are also reassessed when the new information is considered during release planning, updating a product roadmap, iteration planning, or regularly scheduled prioritization sessions.

### 5.3.6 Determining if the Need is Satisfied

At the Initiative Horizon, determining if the need is satisfied is based on assessing if the outputs delivered meet the desired outcome. The decision maker who is responsible for the solution generally makes the decision if the need has been satisfied.

Business analysis practitioners consider if the need has been satisfied every time a solution component has been delivered and feedback has been received on the component. This reduces the risk of producing more output than necessary to meet the need and reduces waste.

Once the desired outcome is achieved, efforts are shifted to meeting the next identified need. If the desired outcome has not been met, business analysis practitioners consider whether to continue, change, or cancel the initiative.

## 5.3.7     Ongoing Assessment of the Viability of the Solution

At the Initiative Horizon, solutions are continually assessed to determine if they are delivering the desired outcomes and sufficient value. Business analysis practitioners base this assessment on both the identified measures of success, as well as feedback received from the Strategy and Delivery Horizons. The decision maker who is responsible for the solution generally makes the decision to continue, change, or cancel the solution.

If the determination is made that the solution is delivering the desired outcomes and sufficient value, efforts continue to refine and deliver solution components.

If the determination is made that the solution is not delivering the desired outcomes and sufficient value, or if there has been a discovery of new information that impacts the solution, business analysis practitioners can:

- change the solution by adding or removing solution components, or changing the priority and sequencing of solution components, or
- cancel the initiative so that resources can be redeployed.

Business analysis practitioners, assess the viability of solutions based on:

- the impact of the current solution on reaching the desired outcomes,
- identified measures of success,
- the anticipated work needed to complete the list of solution components,
- the ongoing assessment of constraints and risks,
- a clarified understanding of the need from the Delivery Horizon, and
- a clarified understanding of the relevance of the need in relation to the broader organizational strategy from the Strategy Horizon.

## 5.4     Time Frame

The Initiative Horizon involves looking into the mid-term future compared to the Strategy and Delivery Horizons. What mid-term means depends on the organization and the context in which it is operating. The time frame for analysis at the Initiative Horizon is mainly determined on how rapidly outcomes are achieved and needs are met. As a general reference, the Initiative Horizon guides analysis and action over the period of the upcoming one to three months. In an agile context, this time frame continually shifts and moves forward, creating what can be considered a rolling time frame.

Although the scope of analysis may be set for the mid-term, ongoing analysis and decisions are central to the success of agile initiatives. As new information emerges and greater clarity and understanding of the need and the solution are achieved, business analysis practitioners apply this learning to the understanding and direction of the solution.

At the Initiative Horizon, business analysis practitioners are driven by the following questions:

- What outcomes are we driving now?

- What outcomes will we be addressing next?

- What outcomes will we be addressing in the future?

These questions can form the basis of a roadmap for the solution.

## 5.5    Feedback and Learning

Decisions made in the Initiative Horizon use feedback from the Delivery Horizon in order to determine whether

- the solution option is still appropriate,

- the selected solution components are still appropriate,

- the solution components are prioritized and sequenced correctly, and

- every solution component needs to be delivered in order to realize the desired outcome.

Delivering continuous small increments of value generates continuous feedback and the learning from that feedback is used to determine if changes in direction are needed.

Decisions made in the Initiative Horizon provide feedback to the Strategy Horizon in terms of changes in the solution that may impact other initiatives currently underway in the organization. For example, if an initiative is cancelled, resources are redeployed in order to satisfy other needs. If a solution needs to change, and that change involves the need for additional resources, there may be an impact on other initiatives.

The Initiative Horizon provides feedback to the Delivery Horizon by indicating the priority and sequencing of solution components.

## 5.6    Applying the Principles of Agile Business Analysis

### 5.6.1    See the Whole

At the Initiative Horizon, the agile principle of See the Whole is applied when decisions to satisfy needs are made. Continuous feedback from both the Strategy and Delivery Horizon inform all the decisions made around solution options, solution components, prioritizing, sequencing, and the viability of the solution.

Business analysis practitioners See the Whole when analyzing which solution components to deliver next because they continually consider the overall strategic need they are trying to satisfy.

The principle of seeing the whole also guides the determination if a need has been satisfied, even if all the solution components have not been delivered. Business analysis practitioners make this assessment based on the identified strategic need, not the output of solution components delivered.

## 5.6.2     Think as a Customer

At the Initiative Horizon, the agile principle of Think as a Customer is applied when the priority and sequencing of solution components are assessed. Business analysis practitioners consider the need from the customer perspective by asking questions such as:

- What would be most valuable to the customer?
- Is there a sequence that would be better for the customer?
- Do I have more than one customer for this solution component?
- Do the answers to any of these questions impact the learning from the other questions?

By thinking as a customer, business analysis practitioners support creating a viable solution with the least amount of output possible.

Thinking as a customer provides a clarity and a greater understanding of the need.

Continuous feedback from customers helps to inform decisions around solution options, solution components, prioritizing, sequencing, and the viability of the solution.

The agile practice of rapid and frequent delivery aligns with the principle of Think as a Customer. By delivering early and often, agile teams quickly obtain real-world feedback from real-world customers of the solution. This learning enhances their understanding of the need and assists with prioritizing and sequencing solution components.

## 5.6.3     Analyze to Determine What is Valuable

At the Initiative Horizon, the agile principle of Analyze to Determine What is Valuable is applied when business analysis practitioners use the shared understanding of the need to identify solution options and prioritize and sequence solution components.

By keeping the concept of valuable outcomes clearly in mind, business analysis practitioners are able to make faster decisions about what solution components to create.

Understanding what is valuable also helps to identify solution components that do not contribute directly to the desired outcome.

### 5.6.4      Get Real Using Examples

At the Initiative Horizon, the agile principle of Get Real Using Examples is applied when establishing a shared understanding of the need, investigating possible solution options, and deciding on the solution to deliver.

Business analysis practitioners start with examples that represent the most common scenarios that customers face. These examples are expanded and refined as the solution is developed. Examples help to verify and validate that the solution still meets the need.

Get Real Using Examples is also valuable when making decisions around solution options, solution components, prioritizing, sequencing, and the viability of the solution.

### 5.6.5      Understand What is Doable

At the Initiative Horizon, the agile principle of Understand What is Doable is applied when prioritizing and sequencing solution components. Understanding what is doable ensures that agile teams do not attempt to deliver solution components that are not possible to deliver within existing constraints.

Business analysis practitioners use feedback from the Delivery Horizon to refine their understanding about what is doable. What was initially thought of as doable may end up to be very difficult, or not worth the effort once the Delivery Horizon starts implementing those ideas.

Understanding what is doable increases efficiency and reduces waste by reducing efforts spent on solution options and solution components that will not satisfy the need because they cannot be delivered.

### 5.6.6      Stimulate Collaboration and Continuous Improvement

At the Initiative Horizon, the agile principle of Stimulate Collaboration and Continuous Improvement is applied when decisions are made based on information provided by a cross-functional team who collaborates to provide the decision maker with timely information relevant to the decision at hand.

In the Initiative Horizon, there is generally a decision maker who is responsible for each decision. Agile teams share the responsibility to provide that decision maker with the appropriate information to make an informed decision.

The agile principle of Stimulate Collaboration and Continuous Improvement is evident when agile teams:

- collaborate to determine whether enough value has been delivered to satisfy the outcome,
- consider whether a solution should continue, change, or be cancelled, and

- conduct retrospectives to discuss how decisions were made, whether all the necessary information informed those decisions, and how to refine the process of making future decisions.

### 5.6.7    Avoid Waste

At the Initiative Horizon, the agile principle of Avoid Waste is applied when business analysis practitioners apply the learning from the agile principle of Understand What is Doable.

Informed decision making is central to the principle of Avoid Waste. When decisions are informed by feedback rather than opinion, they are likely to be more accurate.

Waste is avoided when there is a shared understanding about what outputs will not be delivered because they are not necessary for delivering the desired outcome. Waste is also avoided when initiatives are cancelled when it becomes clear that the solution will not satisfy the need, or when the solution has provided sufficient value to satisfy the need.

# 5.7    Techniques

## 5.7.1    Agile Extension Techniques

- **Kano Analysis**: used to determine the features most relevant to satisfying the identified need and determine the best approach for delivering those features.

- **Personas**: used to create a shared understanding of who the customer is; frequently a core item when Thinking as a Customer.

- **Planning Workshop**: used to create a shared understanding of the approach to constructing the solution.

- **Purpose Alignment Model**: used to determine the features most relevant to satisfying the identified need and determine the best approach for delivering those features.

- **Real Options**: used to understand the appropriate time for making decisions.

- **Relative Estimation**: used to make decisions about which features to deliver and in what order.

- **Retrospectives**: used to provide teams a means of explicitly discussing opportunities for continuous improvement.

- **Story Decomposition**: used to support decisions about which features to deliver, in what order, and how much of the feature needs to be delivered in order to reach the desired outcome.

- **Story Mapping**: : used to elicit and model information about a solution, including notable features or characteristics of that solution.

- **Value Stream Mapping**: used to identify the portions of a problem or solution and identify what their ability is to alter the value of the affected item or process.

### 5.7.2     BABOK® Guide Techniques

- **Backlog Management**: used almost consistently in most agile approaches.

- **Balanced Scorecard**: may provide measures of desired outcomes for the initiative. May be used for "scoring" different solution options or solution components for prioritization.

- **Brainstorming**: used to create many options for a given problem; brainstorming is a technique well suited to agile.

- **Collaborative Games**: used to identify potential solution options.

- **Concept Modelling**: used to build a shared understanding of the need and potential solutions.

- **Data Dictionary**: used to build a shared understanding of the relevant data in the problem and solution space.

- **Data Modelling**: used to elicit information necessary for making the decisions identified in the Initiative Horizon.

- **Document Analysis**: used to elicit information necessary for making the decisions identified in the Initiative Horizon.

- **Functional Decomposition**: used to build and maintain a shared understanding of the desired solution.

- **Glossary**: used to build a shared understanding of the problem and solution space.

- **Interface Analysis**: used to elicit information necessary for making the decisions identified in the Initiative Horizon.

- **Interviews**: used to elicit information necessary for making the decisions identified in the Initiative Horizon.

- **Metrics and Key Performance Indicators (KPIs)**: used to provide measures of desired outcomes for the solution.

- **Observation**: used to elicit information necessary for making the decisions identified in the Initiative Horizon.

- **Prioritization**: used to determine which features will and will not be delivered as part of the initiative and in what order.

- **Process Modelling**: used to build and maintain a shared understanding of the desired solution.

- **Prototyping**: used to create a working or non-working model of a possible solution. Often helps Getting Real With Examples.

- **Risk Analysis and Management**: used to identify information necessary for making Initiative Horizon decisions, especially which features to deliver and in what order.

- **Scope Modelling**: used to build and maintain a shared understanding of the boundaries of th desired solution.

- **Stakeholder List, Map, or Personas**: used to build and maintain a shared understanding of the entities involved with or affected by the solution and its implementaton.

- **Vendor Assessment**: used to provide input into decisions about which solution will satisfy the identified need.

# 6    Delivery Horizon

## 6.1    Purpose

The purpose of analysis at the Delivery Horizon is to inform decisions regarding the delivery of the solution.

## 6.2    Description

Analysis at the Delivery Horizon focuses on the specific aspect of the solution that is currently being implemented. Business analysis practitioners collaborate with team members to ensure there is a shared understanding of the need, identify and prioritize a backlog of actions that will meet the need, and establish a means of assessing outcomes. They do so while seeking to expend the least amount of effort discovering the information necessary to make informed decisions about the solution.

Business analysis practitioners ensure that requirements are mapped clearly to the identified business goals. This involves analyzing and identifying risks, dependencies, and changing needs, and incorporating feedback from customers.

At the Delivery Horizon, business analysis practitioners slice and elaborate upon user stories for the team to implement as working increments of the solution. These increments are added to the backlog. Backlog items are refined into implementable units of business value and elaborated into detail on a just-in-time basis. Immediate feedback from testing and customer evaluation is used to create, alter, re-prioritize, and remove items from the backlog.

## 6.3      Elements

### 6.3.1      Ensuring that User Stories are Ready for Implementation

A user story is well-written when all of the following are true:

the story meets the INVEST criteria (for more information, see <u>7.21. User Stories</u>),

- it contains a well-constructed narrative,
- it presents a set of clear, concise, and precise acceptance criteria,
- it is accepted as representing a desirable unit of implementation,
- it represents an achievable unit of development, and
- it is prioritized clearly in the backlog.

A user story only needs to be ready for implementation when it will be placed into development in the immediate or near future. Refining user stories before they are needed may cause rework and waste because the conditions around the story may change based on ongoing feedback and learning.

### 6.3.2      Maintaining the Backlog

There are two fundamental elements to maintaining a backlog:

- the priority sequencing of items in the backlog, and
- ensuring there are enough items in the backlog to support near-term development efforts.

Business analysis practitioners collaborate with product owners to determine the priority of items in the backlog. The rapid delivery of business value is a central consideration when prioritizing. The sequence of items in the backlog correctly represents their priority order as determined by the product owner.

In order to ensure there are enough items in the backlog to support near-term development efforts, business analysis practitioners collaborate with relevant stakeholders to create features and decompose those features into user stories, which in turn are refined into well-written user stories.

The feedback and learning from the delivered solution impacts the valuation of items in the backlog resulting in continuous change in the backlog. Business analysis practitioners continually re-prioritize, remove, and add items to the backlog. This may happen formally at a backlog refinement meeting or informally as needed in the course of work.

### 6.3.3 Supporting Successful Delivery

Business analysis practitioners work to resolve analysis issues that could interfere with meeting the goals for the current work. Supporting successful delivery means clearing any analysis related roadblocks and applying learning to avoid them in the future.

This can include appropriately handling sequencing and dependencies related to stories, coordinating with external teams and stakeholders, and answering clarifying questions for items currently in the midst of implementation.

### 6.3.4 Ensuring Learning Happens in the Agile Context

At the Delivery Horizon, learning is derived from both processes and the products of those processes, and is framed by the desired outcomes of the immediate work effort. Business analysis practitioners ensure that learning is used to achieve better outcomes. Better outcomes can be described quantitatively or qualitatively.

When deriving learning regarding processes, business analysis practitioners consider what delivery processes should be changed, kept, or stopped in the next delivery cycle. Retrospectives are often used to discuss the learning from the most recent delivery process with the intent of continually improving the delivery process. Information that is too broad, large, or far in the future, can be used as feedback for the Initiative or Strategy Horizons.

When deriving learning regarding products, business analysis practitioners consider if the value delivered in the most recent increment was what was expected. Answers to this question may result in changes to the nature or prioritization of stories for the near-term delivery effort. If the learning suggests the entire initiative or strategy might need to adapt, it can be used as feedback for the Initiative or Strategy Horizons.

### 6.3.5 Maintaining Focus on the Product Vision, Customer, and Value

At the Delivery Horizon, business analysis practitioners apply business analysis techniques and the principles of agile business analysis to retain a focus on delivering the value that is being sought and achieving the product vision.

Constant communication and maintaining a shared understanding of the need and outcomes being sought helps all stakeholders to avoid waste and to efficiently and rapidly deliver value.

## 6.4 Time Frames

At the Delivery Horizon, planning focuses on the day-to-day delivery of backlog items. Agile delivery teams plan on a very short-term basis. What short-term means depends on the organization and the context in which it is operating. As a general reference, the Delivery Horizon guides analysis and action over the period of the upcoming one to four weeks to as long as six to eight weeks. In an agile context, this time frame continually shifts and moves forward, creating what can be considered a rolling time frame.

## 6.5 Feedback and Learning

At the Delivery Horizon, feedback is rapid and ideally in small chunks. Each story delivers a small and rapidly delivered increment of value. Typically, it is not until a collection of stories, delivered over multiple increments, that significant feedback is attained. Business analysis practitioners evaluate the feedback from implemented stories and refine the backlog by identifying what is and is not likely to deliver value. Items in the backlog can be re-prioritized, changed, or removed and new stories can be added based on the reassessment of potential value from the feedback and learning. The agile business analysis principles of Avoid Waste and Analyze to Determine What is Valuable guide the decision making when refining the backlog.

All feedback and learning is considered in the context of the other horizons. If the learning suggests the entire initiative or strategy might need to adapt, it can be used as feedback to the Initiative or Strategy Horizons.

Feedback and learning can occur both in structured processes such as retrospectives or reviews, as well as informally through day-to-day interactions and implementations.

## 6.6 Applying the Principles of Agile Analysis at the Delivery Horizon of Planning

### 6.6.1 See the Whole

At the Delivery Horizon, the agile principle of See the Whole is applied when there is a shared understanding of how individual stories advance the business outcomes and value is created, and there is a means to measure progress against desired goals. Business analysis practitioners ensure that each item in the backlog is prioritized and sequenced in order to contribute to the overall goal of the solution.

During reviews and retrospectives, recommendations for improvement are assessed to determine if they have a positive impact on the overall delivery of the solution.

## 6.6.2      Think as a Customer

At the Delivery Horizon, the agile principle of Think as a Customer is applied when business analysis practitioners align the value being delivered to the customer experiences learned from feedback.

Business analysis practitioners continually consider how both processes and products delivered meet the needs of the customer. Personas (or roles) are frequently used to model and understand customer needs and experiences.

By remaining conscious of who the customer is for each story, and whether or not they would genuinely experience a benefit from the delivery of that story, the business analysis practitioner helps to prioritize items that the customer finds valuable. This contributes to the delivery of the greatest value possible in the shortest time possible.

## 6.6.3      Analyze to Determine What is Valuable

At the Delivery Horizon, the agile principle of Analyze to Determine What is Valuable is applied when continuous feedback and learning is used to maintain the backlog. Business analysis practitioners collaborate with stakeholders to achieve a shared understanding of what is valuable and who derives that value for each story.

Business analysis practitioners analyze what is valuable from both a product and process perspective. From the product perspective, the analysis of feedback and learning guides decisions on maintaining the backlog and refining stories. From the process perspective, consideration is given to what impacts the creation of value:

- Is the team happier?
- Are defects or impediments being reduced?
- Is velocity increased?
- What is the expected benefit of a proposed improvement, and which one might be most important to the team?

## 6.6.4      Get Real Using Examples

At the Delivery Horizon, the agile principle of Get Real Using Examples is applied when examples are used to collaborate when prioritizing stories in the backlog and when creating clear, meaningful acceptance criteria.

Business analysis practitioners use examples to clarify the experience of the customer as they use the story or feature being analyzed.

Examples of specific situations and impacts promote a shared understanding of proposed process improvements and provide clarity when making decisions regarding process improvements.

### 6.6.5    Understand What is Doable

At the Delivery Horizon, the agile principle of Understand What is Doable is applied when need, outcome, constraints, and risks are used to refine and prioritize user stories.

Business analysis practitioners consider their current and evolving understanding of the context to collaborate with stakeholders to achieve a common understanding of what stories or process improvements can actually be accomplished and which ones are not realistically achievable.

### 6.6.6    Stimulate Collaboration and Continuous Improvement

At the Delivery Horizon, the agile principle of Stimulate Collaboration and Continuous Improvement is applied when delivery teams collaborate on analysis and delivery activities as part of their daily work efforts, and during structure review sessions such as reviews and retrospectives.

Collaboration and continuous improvement is a central paradigm in agile business analysis. Business analysis practitioners seek to collaborate and continuously improve in every activity and every interaction with a view to leveraging the variety of strengths present on cross-functional agile teams.

Business analysis practitioners use their skills in problem definition, facilitation, and solution exploration to support process improvement in the delivery of the solution.

### 6.6.7    Avoid Waste

At the Delivery Horizon, the agile principle of Avoid Waste is applied when prioritizing the backlog and focusing on stories that deliver maximum value first, while deferring areas that are not currently of high value.

One of the ways that business analysis practitioners avoid waste is by maximizing the work not done. Directing efforts to the stories that deliver maximum value reduces the efforts directed to activities that do not add the most value to the solution.

## 6.7    Techniques

### 6.7.1    Agile Extension Techniques

- **Personas**: used to create a shared understanding of who the customer is, frequently a core item when Thinking as a Customer.

- **Real Options**: used to understand the appropriate time for making decisions, and the value that each option represents.

- **Relative Estimation**: used to make decisions about which features to deliver and in what order.

- **Retrospectives**: used as a means of explicitly discussing opportunities for continuous improvement.

- **Story Decomposition**: used to decompose epics to stories, which represent incremental work one on solution components.

- **Story Mapping**: used to elicit and model information about a solution, including notable features r characteristics of that solution.

- **Value Stream Mapping**: used to identify the portions of a problem or solution and identify what their ability is to alter the value of the affected item or process.

## 6.7.2 BABOK® Guide Techniques

- **Backlog Management**: used consistently at the Delivery Horizon; backlog management is a frequent if not constant activity.

- **Balanced Scorecard**: used to provide structure to the learning process at this horizon.

- **Brainstorming**: used to create many options for a given problem, brainstorming is a technique well suited to agile.

- **Collaborative Games**: used to help with team building and inspire collaboration with the working group.

- **Concept Modelling**: used to build a shared understanding of the need and potential solutions.

- **Data Modelling**: used to build a shared understanding of the relevant data in the problem and solution space, and as elements of the solution are constructed.

- **Functional Decomposition**: used during the Delivery Horizon in the context of decomposing epics into stories, although the focus is on producing stories which have business value upon completion.

- **Glossary**: used to maintain any terms or definitions that the team may develop or require over time.

- **Interface Analysis**: used to describe a particular user or role using a feature, or how components of the solution will communicate with each other or to outside systems.

- **Interviews**: used to elicit information necessary for making the decisions identified in the Delivery Horizon.

- **Metrics and Key Performance Indicators (KPIs)**: used to trace stories to metrics and the KPIs they are expected to affect.

- **Observation**: used to understand how users perform a task or use the solution.

- **Prioritization**: used to determine which features will and will not be delivered as part of the initiative and in what order. Revisited during the Delivery Horizon periodically or at an emergent need.

- **Process Modelling**: used to represent processes and work that is being done to create or alter those processes.

- **Prototyping**: used to create a working or non-working model of a possible solution.

- **Risk Analysis and Management**: used to make decisions, especially which stories will affect which risks, and in what way.

- **Scope Modelling**: used to build and maintain a shared understanding of the boundaries of the desired solution.

- **Stakeholder List, Map, or Personas**: used to build and maintain a shared understanding of the entities involved with or affected by the solution and its implementation. Personas here can refer to stakeholders around the solution rather than roles, which are more commonly referred to in stories used in solution construction.

# 7 Techniques

The Techniques chapter provides a high-level overview of some techniques commonly used by agile business analysis practitioners.

The techniques described in the *Agile Extension to the BABOK® Guide* are intended to cover the most common and widespread techniques practiced within agile business analysis. Business analysis practitioners apply their experience and judgment in determining which techniques are appropriate to a given context and how to apply each technique. This may include techniques that are not described in the *Agile Extension to the BABOK® Guide*. As the practice of agile business analysis evolves, techniques will be added, changed, or removed from future iterations of the *Agile Extension to the BABOK® Guide*.

## 7.0.1    Selecting the Right Technique

It can be challenging to select the right technique for the situation to get the desired outcome. The following chart provides general guidance on when to choose a specific technique. Please note that many techniques can be used successfully in a variety of contexts. An agile business analysis practitioner uses his or her domain knowledge, experience, individual competencies, and creativity when selecting the appropriate technique for the desired outcome. The purpose of this chart is to provide a starting point when determining which technique might be useful in a given context.

A team is a group of people working together for a shared goal – this team could be at the Strategy, Initiative, or Delivery Horizon. Stakeholders outside the team are customers, subject matter experts, or people internal or external to the organization who are invested in the team's success but are not part of the team.

The context identifies when each technique is most useful to get the desired outcome.

- Communication identifies what techniques facilitate shared understanding, collaboration, and increased communication.

- Process Analysis is about understanding the process to identify ways to improve.

- Product Management or Refinement is about what solution the team is delivering.

- Requirements Management includes techniques specifically helpful in facilitating and improving the requirements life cycle.

- Understanding Your Customer is about identifying, understanding, and clarifying who the customer is and what they need and value.

**Table 7.0.1: Selecting the Right Technique**

| Context | Works well with internal teams | Works well with stakeholders external to the team |
|---|---|---|
| Communications | 7.1. Backlog Refinement<br>7.8. Planning Workshops<br>7.9. Portfolio Kanban<br>7.14. Retrospectives<br>7.24. Visioning | 7.15. Reviews<br>7.24. Visioning |
| Process Analysis | 7.23. Value Stream Mapping | 7.3. Impact Mapping |
| Product Management Refinement | 7.6. Minimal Viable Product<br>7.10. Product Roadmap<br>7.11. Purpose Alignment Model<br>7.12. Real Options | 7.5. Kano Analysis<br>7.6. Minimal Viable Product |
| Requirements Management | 7.2. Behaviour Driven Development<br>7.4. Job Stories<br>7.13. Relative Estimation<br>7.16. Spikes<br>7.18. Story Decomposition<br>7.19. Story Elaboration<br>7.20. Story Mapping<br>7.21. User Stories | |
| Understanding your Customer | 7.7. Personas<br>7.17. Storyboarding<br>7.22. Value Modelling | |

# 7.1        Backlog Refinement

## 7.1.1        Purpose

Backlog Refinement is used to ensure there is enough detail and clarity for items in the backlog so that the delivery team can complete an iteration.

## 7.1.2        Description

Backlog Refinement is a continuous technique used to prepare product backlog items for an agile team to deliver. This is frequently done in preparation for a Planning Workshop. Backlog Refinement incorporates ongoing feedback and learning to revise and refine requirements of needs on an ongoing basis. Refining the backlog based on stakeholder feedback is a critical differentiator for agile initiatives. Backlog Refinement assists the delivery team in delivering a high value, high quality solution within an iteration.

Business analysis practitioners collaborate with team members, stakeholders, and customers to clarify the need and identify additional detail. This can include reviewing priorities with stakeholders and moving or removing items as necessary.

Refinement activities vary based on what is needed to prepare the item for the delivery team. Activities may include Story Elaboration, Story Decomposition, prioritization, and sequencing. Backlog Refinement clarifies which items are high priority for the team to deliver and re-prioritizes or removes unnecessary items.

Backlog Refinement splits large items into smaller ones that meet the INVEST criteria (for more information, see 7.21. User Stories). Acceptance criteria or additional documentation needed to deliver an item can also be added.

Refinement for an item is complete when there is sufficient information for the team to execute.

The outcome of refinement is a common understanding among the team of what is required to deliver the product backlog item (PBI). It also gives the team a chance to look ahead at what is expected next for the solution.

## 7.1.3        Elements

### .1  Backlog

An ordered list of features, requirements, or items needed to achieve the outcomes for the solution. Refinement refers to the activities to keep the backlog relevant and timely for the team.

### .2  Backlog Item

An item on the backlog which represents one or more requirements. Items higher on the backlog are appropriately sized and include enough detail for the team to complete in the next iteration. Items lower on the backlog can be larger and less defined.

Items are most commonly presented as a user story (for more information, see 7.21. User Stories), but can be presented in other formats such as job stories (for more information, see 7.4. Job Stories) or wireframes.

### .3 Refinement Meeting

The purpose of this meeting is for the team to review items that are at the top of the backlog. The outcome of this meeting is confirmation that the top items are ready for the next iteration and identify any further clarity needed. There is no standard format for this meeting, but it is most often led by the product owner or customer representative.

The output of the refinement meeting is backlog items ready for the next iteration.

### .4 Definition of Ready

This is a set of criteria the team agrees must be satisfied to consider an item "ready" for the next iteration. Initially, teams can set the criteria as a critical mass of team members agree the item is ready for the team. As the team reflects and looks to continuously improve, the team may identify additional criteria for their initiative.

## 7.1.4 Usage Considerations

### .1 Strengths

- Increases clarity and common understanding of a product backlog item (PBI).
- Facilitates more effective iteration planning by raising queries early.
- Gives the product owner or customer representative time to answer queries before the team begins executing.
- Ensures product backlog items (PBIs) are sized appropriately for the team.

### .2 Limitations

- Can be inefficient when not aligned to the cadence of the team. If the team reviews the backlog daily as in a flow approach, then refinement should happen whenever a new backlog item is added. If the team reviews the backlog incrementally, then refinement should happen several days before a planning meeting.
- Is usually done by a few members of the team and can inadvertently preclude the views of team members not directly involved in the activity.
- Can be ineffective if the vision and roadmap change frequently.

## 7.2      Behaviour Driven Development

### 7.2.1      Purpose

Behaviour Driven Development (BDD) is used to increase value, decrease waste, and increase communication between stakeholders and delivery teams by focusing on the intended customer behaviour for the solution to satisfy customer needs.

### 7.2.2      Description

Agile values customer collaboration and working solutions to achieve desired output. Agile business analysis practitioners prioritize identifying solutions which deliver customer value in increments. Behaviour Driven Development (BDD) supports that goal through the use of real examples.

Behaviour Driven Development uses a customer readable, domain specific language to specify the intended customer behaviour which satisfies the customer need. It increases speed of delivery by developing only what is needed and creates opportunity for user acceptance test automation. BDD is a technique used to make needs clear and is designed to improve communication and understanding across all stakeholders. Examples are used to understand what the solution needs to do (development) and how to ensure that it does what is needed (testing). The product owner provides the examples and clarifies his or her thinking by doing so. Agile business analysis practitioners identify scenarios by asking "what if" questions in order to expose additional scenarios and express these as additional examples.

Discussions about solution needs are centered on concrete examples that are easily understandable by stakeholders. This leads to a more stable set of requirements than using abstract models alone. The simple format used in BDD leads to direct collaboration between all stakeholders. Collaborative sessions between the product owner, tester, and developer are frequently used. These sessions are known as "Three Amigos" sessions. Close collaboration encourages the delivery team to think like the customer and deliver only what is necessary to achieve this intended behaviour.

The terms Behaviour Driven Development, Acceptance Test Driven Development, and Specification by Example are commonly used interchangeably.

### 7.2.3      Elements

#### .1   Examples

Examples are expressions of real life business scenarios provided by stakeholders. Examples may also be known as scenarios and can be expressed in a number of ways including models. Business analysis practitioners facilitate the discovery of the information which is expressed in the examples and ensure that the set of examples is comprehensive.

Examples are used to discover information about the customer, and not all examples identified will necessarily be within the scope of a development effort.

## .2 Gherkin Syntax

Behaviour Driven Development uses a simple grammar format, referred to as Gherkin, that allows real scenarios to be filled into the syntax. This takes the form:

GIVEN <a situation>

WHEN <an event>

THEN <expected result>

Both GIVEN statements and multiple THEN outcomes for a single scenario could be compound conditions linked with AND statements. There is only one WHEN event that triggers the scenario.

An example for an ATM:

**Scenario 1**: Account has sufficient funds.

- **GIVEN**: I'm in credit
- **AND**: the ATM has sufficient cash available
- **WHEN**: I request $20
- **THEN**: I receive $20
- **AND**: my account balance is reduced by $20

**Scenario 2**: Account has insufficient funds.

- **GIVEN**: I'm in overdraw
- **AND**: the ATM has sufficient cash available
- **WHEN**: I request $20
- **THEN**: I receive no money

Scenarios written in a Behaviour Driven Development format specify events, conditions, and actions are verifiable. They can serve as acceptance criteria for stories and serve as tests in support of Acceptance Test Driven Development that drive a common understanding of requirements and future solution needs.

## .3 Testing

There are several software products that will take examples in this format (but may have their own specific syntax and structure) and allow them to be easily converted into automated tests, thus enabling more agile delivery. Automation of examples enhances and speeds up agile analysis verification and validation activities.

**7.2.4**      **Usage Considerations**

### .1 Advantages

- Behaviour Driven Development (BDD) expresses customer needs in natural language, in a format that all team members can easily understand. The language is based on concrete examples rather than abstract concepts.

- The "Given-When-Then" pattern maps directly onto the "Setup-Execute-Assert" pattern that agile developers use in Test Driven Development. This means the developers can implement the tests directly rather than interpret them.

- The structure of BDD lends itself towards acceptance test automation and supports the production of effective test cases.

- Tools exist to support the use of BDD in projects, and these provide additional metrics such as test case coverage or requirements.

- The automated examples provide the long-term documentation of the system and can be used to demonstrate traceability of requirements for internal stakeholders and external stakeholders such as regulators.

- Scenarios can be easily prioritized which supports the iterative, incremental nature of agile projects.

- Allows flexibility of documentation by creating a lightweight, living requirements and testing document.

- Can be used as acceptance criteria for a user story.

- The Gherkin Syntax can be used to facilitate and structure design discussions to keep the design team focused on a particular behaviour of the system. This is especially the case when the technique is used backwards on a high level design.

### .2 Disadvantages

- It is possible to miss important scenarios unless there is someone who actively asks the "what if" and "what about" questions.

- Where business rules are very complex there could be too many scenarios to easily manage and track without tool support.

- Those maintaining scenarios and test cases must keep them current, relevant, and easy to read to effectively serve their purpose.

# 7.3        Impact Mapping

## 7.3.1      Purpose

Impact Mapping is used to align stakeholders with organizational goals and the creation of customer value.

## 7.3.2      Description

Impact maps align initiatives and delivery activities with overall organizational goals. Impact maps help all stakeholders stay focused on value creation (the why) instead of feature development (the what). Impact Mapping enhances the feedback loops between the Strategy, Initiative, and Delivery Horizons by tying activities to organizational goals.

Impact Mapping is a lightweight approach which shows a big picture view while identifying specific details. In order to ensure the discovery of information from all perspectives, business analysis practitioners generally facilitate a face-to-face brainstorming session.

The impact map is a visual map that breaks down the organizational goals into specific deliverables. This is an example of an impact map:

**Figure 7.3.1: Impact Map**

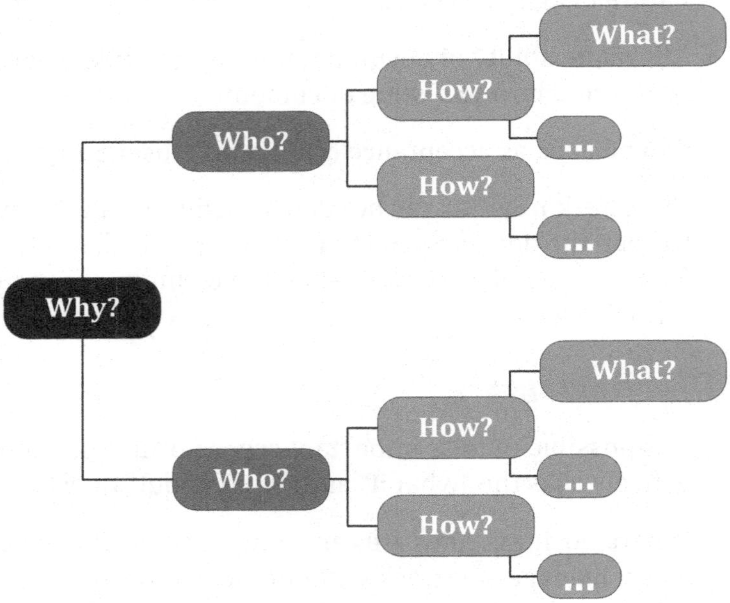

## 7.3.3      Elements

### .1  Components

There are four primary components to an impact map:

- **Goal**: identifies the organizational goals the solution aims to achieve. It answers the question "why are we doing this?"

- **Actor**: identifies the stakeholders who can contribute to achieving the goals. It answers the question "who can influence goals?"

- **Impact**: identifies the actions actors can take to achieve goals. It answers the question "how will actors influence goals?"

- **Deliverable**: identifies which deliverables and functions will help actors achieve the organizational goals. It answers the question "what activities help actors complete goals?"

### .2 Process to Create

Creating an impact map is best done as a face-to-face facilitated exercise to capitalize on the interaction between people of various expertise and knowledge areas. The steps to create an impact map include:

1. Gather all key stakeholders and team members in one space to collaborate.

2. Have space to create the visual impact map.

3. Facilitate the identification of each component, starting with goals, then actors, then impact, and then deliverables.

4. Once the impact map is created, keep it visible for later revision and refinement.

## 7.3.4 Usage Considerations

### .1 Strengths

- Gets the team focused on organizational goals rather than features.

- Reduces waste by preventing scope creep and over-engineered or over-designed solutions.

- Provides transparency to know when business outcomes are achieved and when to stop projects before too much money is spent.

- Impact maps can be created in a short period of time.

- Gives large context with little information.

- The goals or "why" components specify quantifiable objects.

- The visual formats enhance refinement and decision making as new information is found.

### .2 Limitations

- Best done through face-to-face facilitation.

- Impact maps need to be visual, accessible, and can be revised.

# 7.4        Job Stories

## 7.4.1        Purpose

Job Stories are used to represent a product backlog item (PBI) or requirement in terms of a job to be done by a stakeholder.

## 7.4.2        Description

Job Stories focus on the motivation of the stakeholder and provide as much context as possible for the motivations, anxieties, and struggles of the stakeholder. They add contextual information that can affect how a stakeholder wants a desired feature to be and enables helps with making the right implementation decisions.

Job Stories also serve as a communication tool for stakeholders. They facilitate interaction and collaboration among individuals and focus the delivery team on the customer need, while leaving implementation details to be determined.

## 7.4.3        Elements

### .1  Format

A job story follows a specific format. It can be written in first person or third person format.

A job story can be formatted as follows:

> When <situation> I want to <motivation> so I can <expected outcomes>

> When someone <situation>, actor(s) <motivation> so that <expected outcomes>

### Example

**When** I want to withdraw money from my bank account, **I want to** know I have enough money in my account to withdraw some now **so I can** go out to dinner with my friends.

**When** someone wishes to withdraw money from his/her account, **the customer** wants to know if funds are available, **the teller** wants to know if the person banks with us, **so that** the person requesting can received the desired cash amount.

### .2  Situation

The first element of the job story syntax is situation.

Situation provides context for when the job needs to be completed. The context of the situation encourages the delivery team to think of a wide variety of possible solutions. The more context provided, the better the delivery team can design the solution.

When there are multiple roles that would complete a job, those roles are included in the "when" statement.

The persona is not included in the situation specifically so the delivery team can focus on real customers.

### .3  Motivation

The second element of the job story syntax is motivation.

Motivation focuses on the customer motivation. It can include internal and external forces for motivation.

Desired features or solutions are specifically not included in Job Stories in order to focus on the customer.

### .4  Expected Outcomes

The third element of the job story syntax is expected outcomes.

The outcome should satisfy or alleviate the motivation which prompted the situation.

## 7.4.4  Usage Considerations

### .1  Strengths

- This format reduces assumptions regarding the role and removes the persona biases.

- It can be set up for cause and effect scenarios.

- This format focuses on stakeholder motivations instead of defining implementation.

- It is helpful for user experience design.

- Teams find it easier to empathize with the stakeholder.

- Removes focus on features and instead focuses on the stakeholder's desired future state.

- Teams can use Job Stories and User Stories together on backlog. The job story indicates the motivation and outcome for the stakeholder, while the user story indicates features that could solve the problem.

### .2  Limitations

- This format has a tendency to be more verbose than User Stories because of the context, roles, and outcomes included.

- Job Stories can decompose into multiple smaller Job Stories which require management through refinement and prioritization.

- If Job Stories and User Stories are both on the product backlog, teams can get confused when switching between formats.

# 7.5     Kano Analysis

## 7.5.1     Purpose

Kano Analysis is used to understand which product characteristics or qualities will prove to be a significant differentiator in the marketplace and help to drive customer satisfaction.

## 7.5.2     Description

Kano Analysis is a process used to identify features which are viewed by customers as threshold, performance, excitement, or indifferent. This helps determine which features are most important to implement before releasing a solution to market.

Threshold or basic features must be present for customers to be satisfied. These are features they expect.

Performance features customers view as the more the better.

Excitement are features a customer doesn't know they want until they see it.

Indifferent are features the customer doesn't want.

Kano Analysis rates product characteristics on two axes measuring the dysfunctional and functional customer satisfaction for a feature.

The resulting graph is plotted on a matrix. Based on the resulting profile, the product characteristics fall into one of four categories:

- threshold characteristics,
- performance characteristics,
- excitement characteristics, and
- indifferent characteristics.

This analysis can help identify features that will give the solution a unique position in the marketplace based on business value to achieve.

**Figure 7.5.1: Kano Analysis Graph**

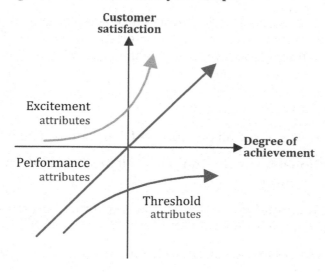

## 7.5.3        Elements

### .1  Threshold Characteristics

Threshold characteristics are those that are absolutely necessary for stakeholders to consider adopting a solution. Their absence will cause intense dissatisfaction but, as they represent minimum acceptance criteria, their presence will not dramatically increase customer satisfaction. The challenge with eliciting requirements for these features is that people expect them to be present and so tend not to think about them unless explicitly asked.

### .2  Performance Characteristics

Performance characteristics are those for which increases in the delivery of the characteristic produce a fairly linear increase in satisfaction. They represent the features that customers expect to see in a solution (speed, ease of use, etc.). Requirements for these types of features are likely to most readily come to mind for the majority of stakeholders.

### .3  Excitement Characteristics

Excitement characteristics are those that significantly exceed customer expectations or represent things the customer did not recognize were possible. Their presence will dramatically increase customer satisfaction over time. As these characteristics are not met by anything currently on the market, stakeholders will not tend to think about requirements that describe them.

## .4  Indifferent Characteristics

Indifferent characteristics are those which add no value to the customer, and the customer does not want. These characteristics are not used. They are not represented on the graph because it will negatively affect customer satisfaction and degree of achievement.

## .5  Determine the Category

Categorization is based on two forms of a question about a feature:

- **Functional form**: How do you feel if this feature or characteristic is present in the product?

- **Dysfunctional form**: How do you feel if this feature or characteristic is absent in the product?

Possible answers to each question form are:

- I like it that way.

- I expect it to be that way.

- I am neutral.

- I can live with it that way.

- I dislike it that way.

The answers are mapped on the functional/dysfunctional grid. The top row represents the answers to the dysfunctional form of the question. The left column represents the answers to the functional form of the question.

**Table 7.5.1: Kano Analysis Questions Grid**

| Functional | | Dysfunctional | | | |
|---|---|---|---|---|---|
| | **Like** | **Expect** | **Neutral** | **Live With** | **Dislike** |
| Like | Q | E | E | E | P |
| Expect | R | I | I | I | T |
| Neutral | R | I | I | I | T |
| Live With | R | I | I | I | T |
| Dislike | R | R | R | R | Q |

## .6  Legend

- E = Excitement

- P = Performance

- T = Threshold

- I = Indifferent (Does not fit into one of the three categories)

- Q or R = Questionable or Reversed (the answer doesn't make sense)

### 7.5.4 Usage Considerations

#### .1 Strengths

- Is applicable for consumer and non-consumer solutions as it focuses on identifying requirements that will encourage widespread use or adoption of a product.

- Analysis can determine feature priority based on the desired position in the marketplace.

#### .2 Limitations

- Only identifies customer satisfaction. Other factors must be included for backlog prioritization.

- The categorization of a particular characteristic tends to shift over time, as customers grow to expect features or characteristics to be present in a product. Excitement eventually become a standard expectation and threshold characteristic (think of the novelty of Google search when first introduced; now customers assume all search responses will be similar).

# 7.6 Minimal Viable Product

## 7.6.1 Purpose

Minimal Viable Product (MVP) is used to avoid cost and risk associated with developing the wrong product by testing a hypothesis, reducing waste, or increasing speed to customers for feedback and adoption.

## 7.6.2 Description

Minimal Viable Product (MVP) identifies the smallest set of features or requirements to deliver value to stakeholders and satisfy early adopters in the shortest time possible. It focuses on core features sufficient to deploy and deliver stakeholder value and no more. Further features are developed after considering feedback from the initial stakeholders.

It applies to

- product development,

- services (commonly to test willingness to pay),

- feature development (to gauge demand), and as

- differentiation (market test strategy).

Minimal approaches are frequently chosen based on time and money constraints. Minimal Viable Product (MVP) enables iterative development cycles by collecting and analyzing feedback before delivering additional features.

MVP generally follows these three high level steps:

**Step 1**: determine the problem to be solved.

- Identify a hypothesis to solve this problem.

**Step 2**: identify a minimum set of features to test the hypothesis of the solution.

- Think about creative, low-cost options to test the hypothesis with the target market.

**Step 3**: analyze validated learning from customers to determine the next step.

- Gather feedback on feasibility of the solution and additional features needed to increase adoption.

## 7.6.3     Elements

### .1 Target audience

Business analysis practitioners clearly identify the target market and who will likely be the early adopters of the solution. Analysis of these groups identifies what problems they may have related to the proposed solution.

### .2 Goal to Achieve or Hypothesis to Test

Business analysis practitioners clearly define the goal or the hypothesis to test with MVP.

For example, the hypothesis may suggest that the new product will lead to quick adoption with the target audience. Or, the organization may hypothesize that a new feature in a product will improve customer service.

### .3 Mechanism to Measure Learning

In order to validate the hypothesis or to determine if the desired goal was achieved, business analysis practitioners identify objective measurements to correlate and interpret the feedback and learning received.

These measurements influence further solution development by identifying the success of the current MVP.

### .4 Defined Requirements

Business analysis practitioners select the minimal amount of requirements necessary to deliver the MVP. This selection is based on the target audience, the goal to achieve, and the mechanism to measure learnings.

The amount of requirements necessary is subjective and dependent on context. There must be enough produced to validate the hypothesis; however, it must be the minimal amount to release the solution quickly.

## 7.6.4     Usage Considerations

### .1 Strengths

- It is less expensive than developing a product with more robust features.

- Reduces cost and risk by gaining customer feedback before engaging in a full solution.

- Avoids building products customers don't want, thereby reducing risk.

- Tests actual usage scenario instead of relying on market research.

### .2  Limitations

- Requires advanced market analysis to identify the necessary feature set for early adopters.

- There is no formula, and desired features are a best guess.

- It is not about creating a minimal product, but testing an initial hypothesis for a product.

- It is not useful for a clear or simple solution. For this situation, the defined Minimal Viable Product (MVP) is the complete product and should be considered as such.

## 7.7  Personas

### 7.7.1  Purpose

Personas are used to understand and empathize with an intended stakeholder in order to align the solution with the stakeholder need.

### 7.7.2  Description

Personas are fictional characters or archetypes that exemplify the way that typical users interact with a solution. They are often used in agile approaches to understand value from the perspective of a particular stakeholder and allow a team that may not have direct access to a customer representative to better understand their needs. Work can then focus on the features of greatest value to a particular persona.

A persona is described as though it is real person. Personas may provide a name, personality, family, work background, skill level, preferences, behaviour patterns, personal attitudes, goals, and needs. They can also include a picture and a short "day in the life" narrative that helps to visualize the user and their experience.

Business analysis practitioners use personas to gain a deeper understanding of stakeholders than is generally provided from a role or actor description. Personas help improve a solution, a purpose, and usability because they are patterned after the subtle qualities of real people that will interact with the solution and how they do their job.

Personas are ranked to identify those that will realize the most benefit from the solution design.

**7.7.3**        **Elements**

**.1  Long and Short Template**

Business analysis practitioners frequently use two different templates when creating personas:

- a short template which offers a one-page quick view of key information, and

- a long template which offers more in-depth details and understanding. Additional user research helps expand from short template to long template.

**Figure 7.7.1: Short Persona Template**

| Name | Details or Context |
|---|---|
| Picture | <ul><li>Tasks and responsibilities</li><li>Technology</li></ul> |
| **Traits and characteristics** | **Goals** |
| <ul><li>Age</li><li>Occupation</li><li>Location</li></ul> | <ul><li>Goal 1</li><li>Goal 2</li><li>Goal 3</li></ul> |

**Figure 7.7.2: Long Persona Template**

| Picture | Name Demographics | Buying motive | |
|---|---|---|---|
| **Traits** | **Needs** | **Motivation** | **Differentiators** |
| | | | |

**.2  Persona Name and Image**

Business analysis practitioners give personas a realistic name and attach a fictional image in order increase its relatability and thereby the understanding of and empathy with the intended stakeholder.

### .3 Traits and Characteristics

Personas include unique, distinguishing, and differentiating characteristics or traits regarding the intended stakeholder.

For example, one ATM persona may be an office manager who deposits cash at the end of the day. A different ATM persona may be an individual who likes to get small amounts out at a time.

### .4 Motivations

Personas include a representation of the underlying motivations regarding how and why the intended stakeholder interacts with the solution.

For example, an ATM office manager may be motivated by reducing risk of fraud or theft. The individual withdrawing from the ATM may be motivated by withdrawing the minimum amount needed.

### .5 Needs

Needs for the persona address very specific needs. These can be basic needs such as safety, trust, or access to food and shelter. They can be higher level needs such as the need for acceptance and validation. Needs are finite as compared to wants which are infinite.

### .6 Differentiators

Differentiators identify specifically why this persona is different from another persona. They identify what is unique about this persona. These could be generational or experiential differentiators, preference differentiators, or identifying characteristics.

## 7.7.4 Usage Considerations

### .1 Strengths

- Personas facilitate the shared understanding of specific requirements for different sets of users. These requirements can be used to develop user stories.

- Proposed solutions can be guided by how well they meet the needs of individual user personas. Features can be prioritized based on how well they address the needs of one or more personas.

- Provide a human "face" so as to focus empathy on the people represented by the demographics.

- If the data is available, using demographic (or anthropomorphic) data about the intended user population is a good way to start building personas. However, in some cases it is necessary to be creative and invent personas based on little more than a few dry facts about the intended end users. In either case, a representative pool of personas should be identified.

- Personas help stakeholders from projecting individual values and biases onto the solution. They help to develop compassion for various users.

### .2 Limitations

- Personas are fictional, so there is a tendency to create personas that embody traits common to most users, but this creates a generic user that is not distinct or realistic. This can lead to solutions that are trying to be everything to everyone.

- Personas may not be a good substitute for a real user. Personas can distance a team from a user community.

- Personas need to be regularly reviewed and updated.

# 7.8 Planning Workshops

## 7.8.1 Purpose

Planning Workshops are used to determine what value can be delivered over an agreed time period.

## 7.8.2 Description

Planning Workshops facilitate the commitment to the delivery of a set of functionality or features within an agreed time period. They enable customer collaboration and response to changes that result from feedback and learning.

Frequently, Backlog Refinement, which involves analysis to get a reasonable gauge of the size, scope, and complexity of each backlog item occurs in preparation for the Planning Workshops.

Typically there are two levels of Planning Workshops:

- one that covers the current release of the solution and takes place prior to the start of iterations, and

- a more detailed session that focuses on work to be done during the iteration or specified amount of the backlog.

Planning Workshops can be used at any planning horizon (Strategic, Initiative, or Delivery). The goal and the level of detail is based on the context of the horizon.

- Planning Workshops at the Strategy Horizon focus on organizational goals, metrics to achieve these goals, and initiatives that can deliver value toward these goals.

- Planning Workshops at the Initiative Horizon produce release plans showing the intended sequence of delivery of user stories or features over the whole release or initiative.

- Planning Workshops at the Delivery Horizon are performed at the beginning of each iteration. In a flow approach, the team identifies the appropriate, regular time to review the next set of backlog items needed to be reviewed. It is important that the team understands and focuses on the iteration objectives, the value associated with a particular minimal marketable feature (MMF), business issues, and story decomposition.

In agile approaches, Planning Workshops are performed on a frequent and regular basis because the solution continually changes based on feedback and learning. Planning Workshops are used to make decisions regarding the prioritization and sequencing based on feedback or changing needs.

In Kanban, the amount of work being performed by the team is limited by restricting the number of work items that can be in any workflow state, not based on iterations. Planning Workshops are used to increase knowledge sharing across the team.

Planning Workshops are organized into two parts:

1. **What**: the product owner discusses the goal, the desired outcome, the date needed, the highest priority backlog items, clarifies specific details, and ensures alignment to goals.

2. **How**: the team discusses how each item can be completed and what is needed for the team to successfully complete them.

## 7.8.3          Elements

### .1  Estimated and Ordered Backlog

Business analysis practitioners provide estimates and order the items in the backlog as a key input to the planning workshop.

### .2  Team Velocity

Prior velocity (throughput capacity of backlog items) is critical to enabling the team to schedule a realistic amount of work. When using Kanban, work-in-progress (WIP) limits will be used to manage this workload instead.

### .3  Iteration Goal or Feature Set

Frequently, an overall goal for the iteration is set to help guide the selection of features. This is a subset of the release goal or roadmap goal. It is an objective that will be met through the implementation of the backlog.

### .4 Backlog Item Selection

At the beginning of the meeting, the iteration goal and the highest priority backlog items are selected from the release plan by the product owner based on organizational value and team velocity. The backlog is composed of feature and non-feature items identified as necessary to achieve the iteration goal or deliver a minimal marketable feature (MMF). For example, there can be bugs to be fixed, a system or environment set up, research initiatives, management work items, or any other activity that adds value to the project.

### .5 Task Planning

Backlog items can be broken down into smaller manageable tasks that can be assigned to specific members of the team.

## 7.8.4 Usage Considerations

### .1 Strengths

- Stakeholders can communicate and collaborate frequently about product vision and evolution of the solution.

- Stakeholders and product owner can guide the solution at every iteration.

- It's easier to understand, estimate, and plan the scope of small iterations instead of the scope of big releases.

- Plans can be changed in advance based on feedback from incremental delivery of the solution.

- Iteration planning can facilitate visibility of the whole solution and synchronization between multiple teams.

- The delivery team can discuss any dependencies between backlog items.

### .2 Limitations

- It is necessary to get all team members together in order to avoid interruptions and rework, especially when working with distributed or concurrent teams.

- If enough time is not set aside to complete the planning workshop, the team will need further conversations to understand the goal and backlog.

- If the solution or backlog items are not well understood during the iteration planning workshop, it is possible it will result in a sub-optimal plan.

# 7.9     Portfolio Kanban

## 7.9.1     Purpose

Portfolio Kanban is used to manage the implementation of strategic initiatives by increasing visibility into the process, work-in-progress (WIP), decision making criteria, and feedback loops.

## 7.9.2     Description

Kanban is a framework which helps in the application of agile values and principles. A portfolio is a collection of strategic initiatives for an organization or department to execute in alignment with their business goals. Portfolio Kanban brings structure to analysis and decision making at the Strategy Horizon.

Portfolio Kanban is a system to manage flow of work during the entire delivery cycle. It focuses on

- visualizing the work,
- limiting work-in-progress (WIP) to increase speed of delivery and reduce waste,
- managing flow by identifying bottlenecks and stalled items,
- making decision making and rules explicit,
- incorporating feedback loops, and
- increasing collaboration and continuous improvement.

The Kanban board visualizes the portfolio to show what initiatives are in progress, identify bottlenecks, and increase visibility to priorities, decision making, and feedback loops. Each portfolio initiative is represented as an item on the Kanban board. Items incorporate metrics or impact goals necessary for decision makers to prioritize initiatives and measure value against business goals.

## 7.9.3     Elements

### .1   Kanban Board

**Columns of Kanban Board**
The columns of the Kanban board represent all the steps identified in the organization to move an initiative or item from idea to completion. For example:

**Table 7.9.1: Kanban Board**

| Waiting to start | Market research and analysis | MVP created for customer feedback | Security review | Productavailable for customers |
|---|---|---|---|---|
| Initiative E | | | Initiative B | Initiative A |
| | | Initiative C | | |
| | Initiative D | | | |

## .2 Done Criteria per Column

For each column or step, there is an explicit criteria indicated when an item is complete and ready to move to the next column. This allows organizations to have a shared understanding of what must be completed to move to the next step.

## .3 Limits per Column

Kanban emphasizes limiting work-in-progress to increase flow through the system. To effectively do this, organizations impose limits for each column based on the reasonable capacity of their departments or teams. The focus is on getting items through the portfolio in a timely manner over having many initiatives in progress without completion.

## .4 Strategic Business Initiatives or Portfolio Items

Each strategic initiative is represented on the Kanban board as a portfolio item. Each item includes a name, short description, and metrics or impact goals to measure success.

## .5 Refinement Meeting

Refinement meetings are used to make decisions and changes based on ongoing feedback and learning. Refinement meetings occur on a regular basis and include all necessary decision makers. Refinement meetings also include those affected by decisions such as product owners for each initiative. There is no standard format for this meeting; the outcomes include a review of the board, analysis of focus areas, and prioritization of existing items.

## .6 Metrics

Each portfolio item includes impact metrics used to prioritize initiatives.

## .7 Visual

One of the strengths of Kanban is providing values into the items on the board. The Portfolio Kanban board is made easily accessible to anyone who wants to view the information. Physical representations that can be easily interacted with have the greatest visibility and lowest barrier to entry.

### 7.9.4     Usage Considerations

#### .1   Strengths

- Can be replicated at the Initiative and Delivery Horizons.

- Optimizes portfolio management to respond to business and customer needs.

- Increases feedback loop per portfolio item and per step.

- Increased visibility into work-in-progress allows people to see current priorities and focus for the organization.

- Increased visibility identifies bottlenecks or impediments which need support.

- Limiting work-in-progress increases overall flow of the system.

#### .2   Limitations

- Useful when all initiatives go through the same flow. It is not useful if there are different paths/columns through which an initiative can move.

- Initiatives should be appropriately sized to regularly move through columns. The approach does not add clarity when initiatives sit in the same column for a long period of time.

- Portfolio Kanban is designed to provide visibility. It is best used for a single flow system. Multiple systems represented on one Kanban board will be overwhelming and not provide the necessary clarity.

# 7.10     Product Roadmap

## 7.10.1     Purpose

Product Roadmap is used to communicate direction and progress towards the vision for a solution or initiative, and it measures progress against that vision through achieving the stakeholders' desired outcome.

## 7.10.2     Description

Product Roadmap is a strategic document and plan used to describe how a product is likely to grow, to align to stakeholders' needs, and to acquire a budget for delivery. It shows features, requirements, or initiatives, and outlines a path to deliver them over time.

Agile values working solutions; product roadmaps focus on product/feature/ value delivered, not milestones or check points.

Product Roadmap enables iterative delivery by expressing features in terms of now, next, and later. It defines what the solution is and what it is not.

**Figure 7.10.1: Product Roadmap**

| Q1 | Q2 | Q3 | Q4 |
|---|---|---|---|
| Capability 1 | | | |
| Capability 2A | Capability 2B | | Capability 2C |
| | Capability 3 | | |
| | Capability 4 | | |
| | | Capability 5 | |
| | | | Capability 6 |

### 7.10.3    Elements

#### .1  Defined Vision and Strategy

Product Roadmap clearly defines the vision and strategy for the initiative. This vision clarifies what is included for the solution and the goal to be achieved. The roadmap also articulates how that vision will be achieved.

#### .2  Defined Desired Outcomes

Product Roadmap clearly articulates organization and stakeholder desired outcomes. Defining the desired outcomes helps the delivery team provide a working solution that adds value.

#### .3  Product Management Team

The product management team is led by the product owner or customer representative. This is a small team focused on maintaining the Product Roadmap. The product management team ensures the roadmap reflects the most current priorities and goals, is accessible to those who need it, and tailors the view based on the audience as needed.

#### .4  Themes

Product Roadmap includes themes which represent a collection of requirements, features, or stories.

#### .5  High-level Requirements

Product Roadmap is comprised of high-level requirements or features which are expected to deliver value to achieve the vision and goals for the solution. These high-level items represent a group of requirements or stories.

**7.10.4**     ## Usage Considerations

### .1 Strengths

- It is visible and accessible to all stakeholders.

- It orients stakeholders to a shared focus.

- It presents a unified view of the solution direction.

- It can be used to facilitate a discussion of options and priorities.

- There can be different views based on the audience for the information. For example, organization executives, solution team, and external customers may have different views of the roadmap.

### .2 Limitations

- Ineffective if the organizational environment leads to a frequently changing vision and desired outcomes.

- Can be misused as a milestone or date-driven roadmap.

- Time-consuming to maintain if overly detailed or multiple different views are required.

# 7.11     Purpose Alignment Model

## 7.11.1     Purpose

Purpose Alignment Model is used to assess ideas in the context of customer and business value.

## 7.11.2     Description

Purpose Alignment Model rates features, processes, products, or capabilities in two dimensions. Business analysis practitioners use this information to help recommend the best actions to improve them based on the ratings.

The first dimension of the Purpose Alignment Model is whether or not the feature creates market differentiation. The second dimension is whether or not the feature is critical for the continued functioning of the organization.

Purpose Alignment Model aids in making ongoing prioritization decisions and focusing investment on those features or capabilities that offer the greatest value to the organization. It was designed for use by for-profit organizations that face competition in the marketplace. Governmental organizations and non-profits use this model with variations aligned to their market goals to drive decisions. Stakeholder value, alignment with the organizational mission, or delivery of social good may serve as an alternative to the market differentiation dimension. The thinking behind the use of the model remains the same even when different labels are used for the dimensions.

Purpose Alignment Model provides guidance on whether something should be an area of strategic concern but does not provide any guidance on what strategies or decisions might be the correct ones.

The following illustration is an example of a Purpose Alignment Model.

**Figure 7.11.1: Purpose Alignment Model**

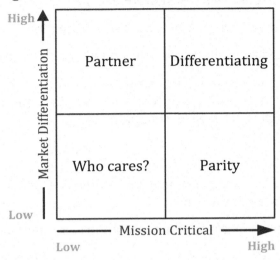

### 7.11.3        Elements

#### .1  Differentiating Quadrant

The differentiating quadrant includes features, products, or services that serve to differentiate the organization in the marketplace and are critical to the functioning of the company. Organizations prepare to invest in these to differentiate from competitor offerings. A differentiating activity might be used to advertise the company, is difficult for competitors to match, or otherwise has significant strategic value, and a unique approach to these activities is likely to be needed.

#### .2  Parity Quadrant

Parity quadrant items are mission critical, but not market differentiating. Many standard functions such as finance, HR, payroll, and others fall into this quadrant for most organizations. Activities in this quadrant are important but do not provide an advantage to the firm in relation to competitors. Adoption of best practices is generally sufficient.

#### .3  Partner Quadrant

Activities in the partner quadrant may have unique value to customers but are not critical to the functioning of the organization. Even though these activities are important to customers or other stakeholders, the organization doesn't need to perform them to survive. That means the organization is unlikely to have the resources to excel at these activities (as more mission-critical operations will take precedence), while a partner may perform them more effectively.

### .4  Who Cares? Quadrant

Activities which are neither mission-critical nor help to differentiate the organization in the marketplace fall into the who cares? quadrant. As these activities do not add customer value, and the organization can function without performing them, they are prime candidates to be eliminated and the resources reallocated to support more useful work.

## 7.11.4  Usage Considerations

### .1  Strengths

- One of the key advantages of this technique is its simplicity. It can be taught to business sponsors and users in a couple of minutes, so they can critically assess an idea themselves.

- The model is easy to use in a facilitated, collaborative environment.

- It can be applied at any horizon.

- It enables analysis in a short time frame.

### .2  Limitations

- It assumes positive intent in the business strategy.

- The participation of the right stakeholders is necessary for success.

- The simplicity of this technique can omit or overlook an important nuance for a feature.

# 7.12  Real Options

## 7.12.1  Purpose

Real Options is used to help determine when to make decisions.

## 7.12.2  Description

Real Options address aversion to uncertainty by providing the conditions when a commitment should be made rather than simply suggesting to wait or make the decision too early. Real Options helps stakeholders to delay decisions to the last responsible moment and focus on the highest priority item.

Real Options reduces the number of decisions to consider at any one time and delays decisions about the detail of requirements as long as possible. This is achieved by treating the detail of requirements as options and the commitment point as the time to elaborate on details. Real Options delays making decisions or commitments until the last responsible moment when the decision needs to be made.

Real Options has three simple rules:

1. options have value,

2. options expire, and

3. never commit early unless you know why.

Options have value means keeping options available and provides value through flexibility to respond to feedback, learning, and changing needs.

Options expire means that decisions do need to be made at a certain point. Options with no expiration provide no value as that implies a decision never needs to be made.

Never commit early means keeping options available to the last responsible moment to encourage feedback, learning, and the opportunity to change.

Real Options is frequently used as a refinement and prioritization technique. It indicates when a decision should be made and when more details are needed. For iteration initiatives, this occurs during the next planning session. For flow initiatives, it occurs the next time capacity becomes available to work on something new.

## 7.12.3  Elements

### .1  Options

A key element of this technique is the options themselves.

Examples of options include:

- A user story: an option to implement a piece of functionality. The option expires when the business need changes.

- Acceptance criteria: an option to include a certain level of detail for a user story.

- A hotel reservation: an option to stay at the hotel. The option normally expires at 6 p.m. on the day of the stay at which point you are committed to paying for the hotel room.

- A business card: the option to contact the person who gives you the card. The option expires when the person changes contact details.

Examples of items that are not options include items or activities that

- you cannot do,

- you cannot afford,

- you cannot do in time,

- you cannot buy or sell, and

- you do not have the tools for.

Options are available until a point in time. They can be committed to or not. Once committed, the other options expire. Often, there is a penalty associated with failing to meet a commitment.

### .2 Commitments

Some examples of commitments include:

- Using the organization's standard software development language to build a product. Failure to meet this commitment introduces risk and maintenance costs to the organization.

- Acceptance criteria completed prior to the Planning Workshops.

Turning up to work on time. Failure to meet this commitment may result in termination of your contract of employment.

Delivering items from the backlog that you have committed to deliver. Failure to meet this commitment will reduce trust and damage the team's reputation with customers.

### .3 Options Expiry

In Real Options, the expiry date is conditional. This expiry date forces consideration of when options expire and no choice can be made.

Determination of when an option expires is the most important aspect of Real Options. This knowledge is critical to prevent making decisions too soon or too late.

### .4 Right/Wrong/Uncertain

Business analysis practitioners strive to provide quality information that supports making the right decisions. In a rapidly changing context, decision makers face much uncertainty. Frequently this uncertainty causes decisions to be made too early. If a decision is made too early, there is an increased chance that the decision will be the wrong decision.

Business analysis practitioners use Real Options to determine when information is needed to make a decision (right before the first option expires) and then gather information up until that point to improve the chance of being right.

## 7.12.4 Usage Considerations

### .1 Strengths

- Simplifies decision making by providing a simple set of information to follow.

- Enables faster decision making because the focus is on the immediate decisions and defers prioritization until later when complexity is resolved.

- Informs when, not how, to construct decisions, which makes them broadly applicable as an approach.

- Optimizes processes by forcing the consideration of the decision points and the information arrival process (when data arrives and whether it arrives before the decision).

### .2 Limitations

- Can be counterintuitive as they require analysis of systems from the outputs to the inputs.

- Are not a simple process to be followed by rote. It is a complex technique which requires practice and study.

## 7.13 Relative Estimation

### 7.13.1 Purpose

Relative Estimation is used to make future predictions based on past experience, knowledge, complexity, size, and uncertainty required to complete backlog items.

Estimation is discussed at length in the *BABOK® Guide*: 10.19 Estimation. The *Agile Extension to the BABOK® Guide* builds on the information in the *BABOK® Guide* and describes relative estimation techniques that can be applied in an agile context.

### 7.13.2 Description

In an agile context, estimating is progressive and occurs in alignment with iterations. Initial estimates are not expected to be as accurate as latter estimates provided closer to delivery. The ability to accurately estimate improves over time as new information is discovered about both capacity and capabilities. The continuous feedback and learning that is central to agile business analysis provides clarity and understanding regarding the components, characteristics, and complexity of the work.

Estimates are not part of the solution and are used to guide internal decision making. Estimates provide value to stakeholders by

- determining cost and effort,

- establishing the priorities of the initiative, and

- committing to a schedule.

In addition to the basic approach of estimating based on historical knowledge, agile business analysis practitioners frequently apply a relative estimating model in which teams develop stories that define user needs and benefits. These stories are analyzed and numeric values are applied to each story as story points. Story points apply a Fibonacci scale to abstract measurement of factors indicative of story size. Relative estimation is based on the team's past experience and will vary between teams.

A story point is a relative number assigned to each story that defines the estimated effort a team will have to apply to deliver the story. Story points are usually based on what the team knows about the story in five key areas:

- **Knowledge**: How much information does the team have?

- **Experience**: has the team done this/similar item before?

- **Complexity**: How difficult is the implementation likely to be?

- **Size**: How big is the story? How long will it take?

- **Uncertainty**: What variables and unknown factors might impact the story?

The total number of story points delivered within any given iteration is considered to be the team's velocity, or how much a team accomplished within the iteration. Over several iterations, teams will have a better understanding of their actual velocity. This allows them to make better informed estimates and commitments in subsequent iterations.

### 7.13.3 Elements

There are several ways to estimate story points. Business analysis practitioners begin with

- an order of magnitude,

- a given set of resources and a fixed iteration, or

- a team based estimation of the time required for a sample of stories of different sizes, and then extrapolate from there to estimate the work that can likely be done in an iteration.

### 7.13.4 Approaches

#### .1 Planning Poker

Planning poker is a technique to estimate story points for a team. During the Planning Workshop, the team reviews each backlog item or story. Once the team has a shared understanding of the story, each team member chooses a number based on the story point scale. Where alignment is within one degree of numbers, the team chooses one and moves on. Where there is a wide variation in numbers, the team discusses the discrepancy to uncover any assumed knowledge. The goal is for the team to reach agreement for each story point during the Planning Workshop.

#### .2 Silent Sizing

Silent sizing is an approach which engages the entire team in estimation activities. To do this, the team needs backlog items prepared on individual cards and a wall, table, or similar space to line up the items. Taking turns, a team member selects a card and places it along the wall. The team members repeat this for all cards, creating a linear line with the smallest cards on one end and the largest cards on the other end. The team then identifies breaking points to group similar sized items. At this point, the team assigns a number, such as the

Fibonacci scale, to each grouping. Each card is assigned the size of its group.

### 7.13.5 Usage Considerations

#### .1 Strengths

- A simple, reliable methodology that fits well with agile practices. It is highly adaptive and is likely to become increasingly accurate throughout successive iterations.
- The sizing approaches are highly collaborative and based on consensus, and will likely have a positive impact on development teams.

#### .2 Limitations

- Relative estimates are based on historical data, and accuracy is dependent upon the similarity of new stories to stories previously delivered. If new stories differ radically from previous stories, it is possible that the accuracy of the estimate may decrease.
- The accuracy of velocity is dependent on the knowledge and experience of the development team working together. Any changes to team composition will impact velocity and therefore future estimates.
- Numbers used are team specific, and comparisons between teams can lead to confusion for stakeholders.
- Relative estimates can be misconstrued as a definitive time to complete.
- Stakeholders outside the team may focus on the estimates (output) instead of value delivered (outcomes).

## 7.14 Retrospectives

### 7.14.1 Purpose

Retrospectives are used to continuously improve by reflecting on what went well, what could be better, and to improve the processes.

### 7.14.2 Description

The retrospective provides an opportunity for all members of the team to reflect on the most recent deliveries. The retrospective includes the entire team. It is common for the retrospective to be split into two parts. First, the team reflects on the past iteration. Second, the team identifies ways to adapt.

Retrospectives are held at key milestones in the solution life cycle, normally at the end of every iteration/release, so learning can be quickly embedded in the processes and practices going forward.

Retrospectives focus on identifying issues with the process. They identify process improvements and are not personal in any sense. They include a safety check to ensure team members can speak freely and constructively.

It may be useful for Retrospectives to be facilitated by a neutral facilitator rather than by a member of the team.

Where fixed iteration cycles are not being used, regular Retrospectives are scheduled to enable the team to examine their processes.

## 7.14.3        Elements

### .1 Review Previous Action Items

During a retrospective, action items identified in the previous retrospective are reviewed, and progress and impact assessed.

### .2 Preparation

The team prepares ideas from the recent iteration that may be analyzed in the retrospective.

### .3 Safety Check

The team agrees, together, to trust each other and to believe every comment or suggestion is intended for the sole purpose of improving the team's performance.

### .4 Identify the Items

There are many mechanisms to identify items to discuss. One of the most common is for all team members to write up things that went well, things to improve, and things of interest to share as a group.

### .5 Choosing Future Actions

Once all the ideas have been discussed to the satisfaction of the team, the team decides which solutions or improvements to focus on next. The team then identifies a timeline and assigns responsibility to an individual team member who ensures the solution or improvement is implemented.

## 7.14.4        Usage Considerations

### .1 Strengths

- An excellent way for the team to find a collective voice around opportunities for team improvement.

- Addresses issues early and focuses on improving the process.

- Allows continuous improvement of the team.

- Empowers the team.

- Can be self-facilitated by the team.

### .2  Limitations

- Team members may feel obliged to pretend that they trust each other, even though they do not.

- Retrospectives are only of value if the team acts upon the learning from the session to improve the process.

- Most ideas raised in the retrospective are known to at least one member of the team. A mature team should be addressing issues as they arise rather than batching them up to be handled in a retrospective.

If issues raised in the retrospective are not addressed, there is a risk to team morale and motivation.

# 7.15        Reviews

## 7.15.1      Purpose

Reviews are used to demonstrate and inspect an increment of the solution with stakeholders in order to elicit feedback to determine if the solution being developed aligns with the need.

Reviews are discussed at length in the *BABOK® Guide*: 10.37 Reviews. The *Agile Extension to the BABOK® Guide* builds on the information in the *BABOK® Guide* and describes how Reviews are applied in an agile context.

## 7.15.2      Description

Reviews showcase or demonstrate a working solution in order to solicit feedback. This can be done formally or informally with stakeholders. Reviews are led by the team who completed the work. They focus only on completed work. Reviews are most successful when they tie the work to the vision, objectives, and goals for the organization and initiative.

Eliciting feedback early and often is a core element of agile business analysis because it increases the chance for a solution to satisfy the need when delivered to customers. Reviews bring key stakeholders together for a face-to-face conversation about completed work. It empowers the team through direct feedback solicitation.

This is an opportunity for the product owner or customer representative to solicit stakeholder feedback. They synthesize feedback to determine the next features to prioritize and which feedback to incorporate into the backlog. Product owners provide feedback to the team throughout the iteration with each item delivered.

### 7.15.3      Elements

#### .1   Solution Being Delivered

Reviews demonstrate an increment of the completed solution that is being delivered. This provides something tangible to which the stakeholders can react and provide feedback.

#### .2   Stakeholders

Reviews include:

- **Key Stakeholders**: this includes stakeholders best able to give feedback on whether the completed increment delivers a solution which satisfies the need.

- **Team**: all team members working on the initiative are present to facilitate discussion and elicit feedback.

- **Product Owner/Customer Representative/Product Manager**: the decision maker who leads the initiative and is responsible for ensuring Reviews solicit feedback on the solution from stakeholders.

### 7.15.4      Usage Consideration

#### .1   Strengths

- Elicits feedback in an informal manner from stakeholders.

- Lightweight facilitation and conducted on a regular cycle.

- Serves as a check point for the team to validate whether they are on track to deliver the solution when needed.

- Face-to-face communication is preferred.

- Engage stakeholders as early as possible.

- Continue regular engagement with stakeholders during the Delivery Horizon.

#### .2   Limitations

- If Reviews include a wide range of stakeholders, feedback can be too varied for the team to analyze and act upon effectively.

- If hierarchy is highly valued within an organization, higher ranked stakeholders' feedback could be considered more important than other feedback, regardless of their interaction and understanding of the product or service goals.

# 7.16        Spikes

## 7.16.1        Purpose

Spikes are used to time-box research, design, exploration, investigation, or prototyping activities in order to understand the effort required to deliver a backlog item or an initiative.

## 7.16.2        Description

When a backlog item or initiative that cannot be estimated is identified, business analysis practitioners use Spikes to gain the knowledge necessary to estimate what is required to deliver the backlog item or initiative.

Spikes are time-boxed activities that have clear objectives and desired outcomes. Spikes are exploratory in nature and do not produce a potentially shippable product. This includes exploring different potential approaches to a problem including researching different interfaces or tool options.

Spikes are often technical, and may be done to prototype a solution approach to the feature. This technique allows delivery teams to learn how to deliver a working product effectively and efficiently.

## 7.16.3        Elements

### .1  Spike Goal

Each spike has a defined goal or outcome in order to define when the purpose has been completed. Business analysis practitioners define a specific time-box to devote to this spike within an iteration.

### .2  Type of Spike

There are three types of Spikes:

- **Functional**: analyzes a story and determines how to break it down into smaller stories or tasks, or identify where the risk and complexity exists.

- **Technical**: determines feasibility or impact of a story or task to understand the technical design necessary.

- **Exploratory**: explores organizational risks or impacts for a particular initiative or backlog item.

## 7.16.4        Usage Considerations

### .1  Strengths

- Specific activities and time-box provides focus for the team to get clarity.

- Gives permission to spend time on value-driven research.

- When used early in team formation, can help team members build and share knowledge about each other and the technology to be used for the solution.

### .2  Limitations

- Can be too long a time-box or too large an item to have clear objectives and outcome.

- The term can be incorrectly used to reference follow-up conversations.

- If used too frequently, this indicates the product backlog refinement is not meeting team needs.

## 7.17        Storyboarding

### 7.17.1      Purpose

Storyboarding is used to describe a task, scenario, or story in terms of how stakeholders interact with the solution.

### 7.17.2      Description

Storyboarding (also known as dialogue map, dialogue hierarchy, customer journey, or navigation flow) is a technique for understanding how people will actually use the solution. Storyboarding is used in conjunction with other techniques such as use cases, user stories, and prototyping to detail visually and textually the sequence of activities summing up different user interactions with the solution.

Storyboarding is used when formal prototypes may be unnecessary or too expensive.

Storyboarding serves

- to elicit, elaborate, organize, and validate the requirements,

- to communicate to stakeholders what needs to be built,

- to assist in user interface design,

- to show different variations of the proposed solution,

- to align stakeholders with the vision of the proposed solution, and

- as an input to tests.

When used to describe the interaction with a software system, the storyboard shows how screens will look and how they will flow from one to another. When used to describe the business organization, the storyboard shows the interaction with a business process such as back office.

Storyboards can be developed as either physical or digital products and can be created in a workshop environment with relevant stakeholders.

Storyboards are common in many analysis and development approaches, and are a form of prototyping (see *BABOK® Guide:* 10.36 Prototyping). Storyboards present all the details in a visual flow. In contrast, story maps (see 7.20. Story Mapping) is an organization of user activities.

**Figure 7.17.1: Storyboard**

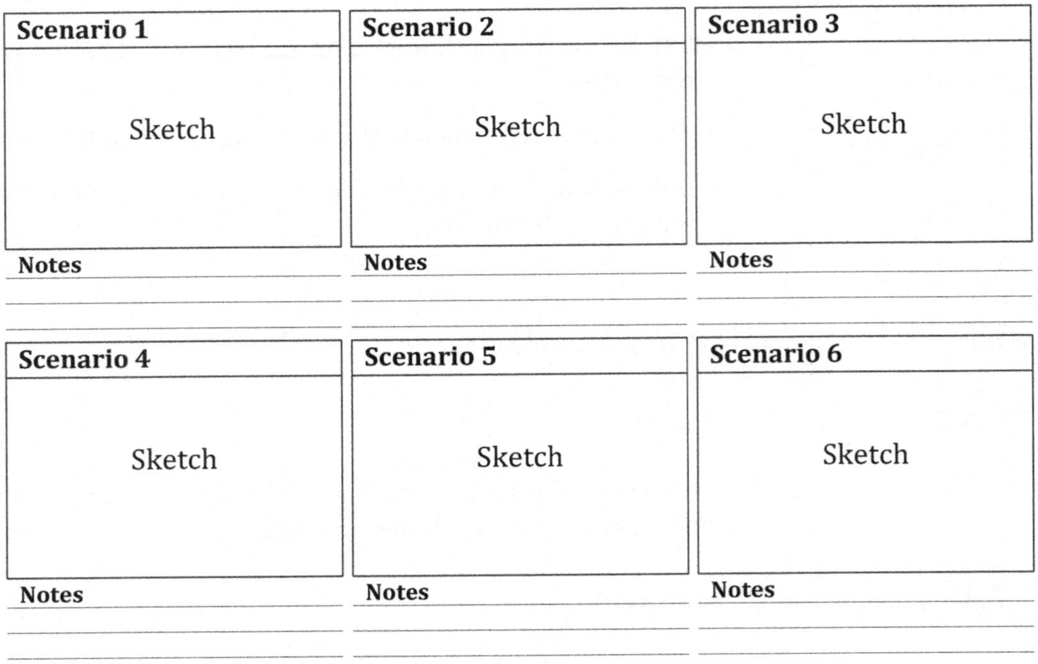

| Scenario 1 | Scenario 2 | Scenario 3 |
|---|---|---|
| Sketch | Sketch | Sketch |
| Notes | Notes | Notes |

| Scenario 4 | Scenario 5 | Scenario 6 |
|---|---|---|
| Sketch | Sketch | Sketch |
| Notes | Notes | Notes |

## 7.17.3          Elements

### .1  Scenarios

When planning a solution, business analysis practitioners identify all the possible scenarios for which a customer will interact with the solution. They consider the nuance of each scenario, which steps the customer will take, and what is the desired outcome. The likelihood of the scenario occurring and the complexity involved in the scenario is also identified.

### .2  Illustrations

Storyboards are visual illustrations of the solution and how the customer interacts with it. Typical storyboards involve a series of boxes or segments depicting each step in the scenario.

### .3  Textual Explanation

To add context to the visual illustrations, textual explanations accompany each box or segment to explain the step as necessary.

### .4 Create Storyboard

The steps to creating a storyboard include:

1. Identifying the main scenarios within the scope of the initiative. This can be derived from use cases, user stories, in a customer visit, or an information gathering session with subject matter experts.

2. Selecting the scenarios for the storyboard. Not all scenarios require a storyboard. The most common and most complex scenarios are storyboarded.

3. Creating illustrations for the storyboards of the selected scenarios.

4. Enhancing the storyboard illustrations with textual information such as optional interactions, unavailable interactions, further stakeholder requests not associated with the primary scenario, and general notes associated with a specific step. Each storyboard should stand on its own with required explanations.

5. Validating the storyboard with stakeholders to ensure accuracy and alignment.

## 7.17.4 Usage Considerations

### .1 Strengths

- Can significantly reduce abstractness caused by other techniques such as use cases and user stories.

- Can be produced quickly and at a very low cost compared to other techniques such as prototypes.

- The intuitive nature of the storyboard encourages stakeholder participation.

### .2 Limitations

- Different look and feel than the final product.

- Easy to get bogged down on how, rather than why.

- Easy to miss some significant rules or constraints due to concentration on the visual flow.

# 7.18 Story Decomposition

## 7.18.1 Purpose

Story Decomposition is used to represent the requirements for a solution at the appropriate level of detail and are aligned to desired outcomes.

**7.18.2**          ## Description

Story Decomposition provides a structure for defining the various elements of requirements at progressively smaller levels of granularity, starting with the broad system context and drilling down in multiple levels to eventually define the detailed acceptance criteria for individual stories.

Any story that is too large or insufficiently understood to elaborate, estimate, or deliver as a story is ready for decomposition. The most common agile approach to story decomposition can be described as "breadth-before-depth":

- the decomposition first describes a high-level view of what business goals need to be achieved,

- the high-level view is decomposed into smaller components that provide increments of customer value (sometimes called minimal marketable features or MMFs), and

- these smaller components are decomposed into stories, and the stories are elaborated into smaller increments with acceptance criteria (see 7.19. Story Elaboration).

Story Decomposition is undertaken progressively. In agile initiatives, the initial analysis activities identify the goals, MMFs, and most of the large stories. The initial decomposition of stories is completed incrementally. There is an implicit understanding that these stories are likely to change and that the understanding of the requirements will evolve over time. Therefore, decomposing to the lowest level of detail is likely to be a wasteful activity early in the initiative.

**Figure 7.18.1: Story Decomposition**

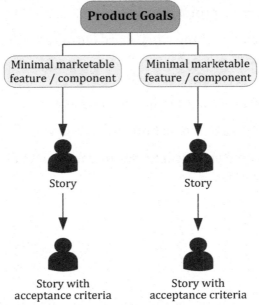

Story Decomposition is applied in different ways depending on context. For example, some business analysis practitioners follow the model linearly, as shown in the above diagram, while others use techniques that work best in their environment. Once the MMF or feature groups have been developed, use cases may be used instead of stories. Business analysis practitioners focus on dynamic collaboration, facilitation, and communication in getting acceptance for the minimum required detail to develop and deliver the solution.

## 7.18.3      Elements

### .1  Solution Goals

The solution goals are the highest level of business requirements. They represent the business drivers for undertaking the initiative and form the rationale against which all of the detailed level needs are assessed.

### .2  MMF/Component

Minimal marketable features are logical groupings of functionality and capabilities the delivered solution needs to provide to be worth releasing. Often these will form the themes for a single release and serve to provide a big picture context for the product being developed.

### .3  Story

Represents a user story, job story, use case, or requirement to be implemented in the delivered solution.

### .4  Acceptance Criteria

Conditions of satisfaction or criteria needed to validate a user story. Can be written as lists of items, specifications, or user acceptance tests (or a combination). Detailed requirements are represented and validated in the acceptance criteria.

## 7.18.4      Usage Considerations

### .1  Strengths

- Helps avoid the common problem of getting lost in the detail of the user stories and losing the big picture context.

- It is important that team members keep the project's goals and objectives in mind and can trace implemented or requested functionality back to the driving business objectives.

- Breaking the product into MMFs and epics helps with release-level planning, provides visibility into the development of the solution, and helps coordinate external program activities such as organizational change management and user training.

### .2  Limitations

- A common anti-pattern is the temptation to treat Story Decomposition as a way of reverting to detailed requirements upfront. Ensuring the continued emphasis on just-enough and just-in-time means knowing when to stop decomposing.

- Story Decomposition should not be done based on process (step 1, 2, and 3 in a flow), architecture (build database, build server, build front-end), or procedure (design it, build it, test it). Rather, decomposition should be done based on customer valued features.

# 7.19          Story Elaboration

## 7.19.1       Purpose

Story Elaboration is used to define the detailed design and acceptance criteria for a story as needed to deliver a working solution.

## 7.19.2       Description

Story Elaboration is the lowest level of Story Decomposition and the process by which the story is broken down into pieces of work. Story Elaboration facilitates the elicitation and communication of the most detailed requirements.

Story Elaboration is an ongoing activity which occurs in the Delivery Horizon (for more information, see 6. Delivery Horizon). Wasted effort is reduced by elaborating stories on a just-in-time and just-enough basis. Business analysis practitioners continually develop and communicate dynamic requirements, and this necessitates a high degree of skill in both facilitation and communication.

During each iteration, time is scheduled to expand on the story to understand the detail. Often, this is completed in a workshop with those who will execute the story: subject matter experts, the customer representative who needs the story, the person who will test the story, and a business analysis practitioner who facilitates and challenges the story. Story Elaboration is completed in preparation for the Planning Workshop (for more information, see 7.8. Planning Workshops).

In order to ensure detailed requirements include the most current feedback on learning, Story Elaboration is done on a just-in-time basis for stories that have been determined to be in scope for the upcoming iteration.

## 7.19.3       Elements

### .1  Elicitation

Elicitation is the drawing forth or receiving of information from stakeholders or other sources.

### .2  Story Decomposition

Story Elaboration can identify opportunities to decompose stories (for more information, see 7.18. Story Decomposition).

### .3  Acceptance Criteria

Story Elaboration clarifies, adds, or removes acceptance criteria for a story (for more information, see *BABOK*® *Guide*: 10.1 Acceptance and Evaluation Criteria).

### .4  Additional Optional Elements

Story Elaboration may identify tasks to deliver the upcoming iteration. These outputs may include

- task definitions and breakdowns,
- examples and scenarios to explain the customer's intent for the story,
- low-fidelity models to clarify the technical or process design (for example, data models and data flow diagrams),
- screen or report mock-ups, and
- input/output data tables.

### .5  Outcome

The result of Story Elaboration is a shared understanding among stakeholders of what should be delivered to achieve the "Done" state for this story.

## 7.19.4        Usage Considerations

### .1  Strengths

- Reduces elicitation time, and potentially less documentation, by focusing on current features.
- Elaborating requirements only as needed helps the team avoid the work of eliciting requirements for features that will change by the time they are ready for implementation.
- Keeps the team focused on the highest priority feature.

### .2  Limitations

- Incomplete elaboration can lead to too many or too few details for a story to be completed.
- Proper timing is difficult. If conducted too early, the information may no longer be correct for the given release and will need to be re-elicited. However, when collected too late, it can delay project team progression to development.
- It can be challenging to elicit the appropriate level of detail such that the requirements can be developed, tested, and compared to acceptance criteria.

# 7.20    Story Mapping

## 7.20.1    Purpose

Story Mapping is used to assist in creating understanding of product functionality, the flow of usage, and to assist with prioritizing product delivery.

## 7.20.2    Description

Story Mapping provides a visual and physical view of the sequence of activities to be supported by a solution. It uses a two-dimensional grid structure to show sequence and groupings of key aspects of the product on the horizontal dimension, with detail and priority of stories on the vertical dimension. Story Mapping is a decomposition technique which allows for the evolutionary understanding of a solution starting with an end-to-end view and drilling down to the detailed user stories.

Story Mapping is an effective tool to help understand the need while focusing on the highest priority items for analysis.

A story map is designed to be an information radiator, used to visualize a solution's outcomes in the context of usage and priority. The story map is often placed on display for the delivery team during release planning sessions. By analyzing the story map, business analysis practitioners can more readily identify dependencies generated as a result of the intended flow through the user stories. The story map can also be used for risk assessment and management by examining how the stories will need to work together in the context of delivering business value.

The following illustration is an example of a story map.

**Figure 7.20.1: Story Map**

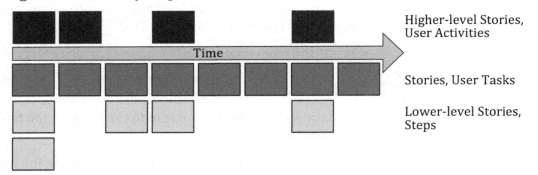

**7.20.3**          **Elements**

### .1 Themes or Activities

The top line of a story map features all known themes or activities a customer will follow in a linear path. For example, themes for using an ATM could look like:

1. Activate machine.

2. Validate account credentials.

3. Perform request.

4. Receive outcome.

5. Choose completion or another transaction.

These themes are a broad view of all activities for all known personas.

### .2 Stories or Features

Underneath corresponding themes, individual stories or features are featured. These include all known features related to a theme. Each story may apply to only one persona or more than one persona.

### .3 Ranked Priority Order

Stories are arranged top down under each theme in priority order. This allows for the separation of features between releases. A ranked priority order identifies the stories which appeal to the most and highest ranked personas as well as the personas that are required to be implemented before subsequent features.

### .4 Facilitation

Story Mapping is a self-facilitation technique. No dedicated facilitator is required to develop a story map. Frequently, Story Mapping is a group activity to prioritize current stories, identify missing stories, and select stories for story elaboration (for more information, see 7.19. Story Elaboration) and story decomposition (for more information, see 7.18. Story Decomposition). A product owner can assist the group by making decisions when needed.

Themes and stories are prepared in advance of the Story Mapping session to focus the team effort on prioritization and understanding the customer's path.

### 7.20.4      Usage Considerations

#### .1   Strengths

- When the larger context of a solution is not accounted for, agile projects can be subject to getting mired in the details with an inability to effectively string components together to create end-to-end business value. Story maps help avoid the common problem of getting lost in the detail of the user stories and the risk of losing the big picture context.

- Story maps include personas to help the team prioritize based on features most relevant to one or more specific personas.

- Story maps can also be used to understand the flow of data within a system.

#### .2   Limitations

- Story maps can become cumbersome when the solution is very large and may require building a number of story maps that cover a large program of work. While story maps illustrate a flow, they do not analyze or illustrate dependencies between requirements. They can be used to help facilitate that analysis.

- Contexts that are not process oriented may find story maps less useful.

## 7.21      User Stories

### 7.21.1      Purpose

User Stories are used to convey a customer requirement for the delivery team.

User Stories are described in detail in the *BABOK® Guide*: 10.48 User Stories. The *Agile Extension to the BABOK® Guide* builds on the information in the *BABOK®* and describes how User Stories are applied in an agile context.

### 7.21.2      Description

User Stories are a representation of the customer need and are expressed as a small, concise statement of a feature needed to deliver value. User Stories facilitate the interaction and collaboration of stakeholders.

The user story expresses a customer need and value desired. Typically, they are one or more sentences written by the customers, product owners, or business analysis practitioners which describe something of value to a stakeholder. User Stories provide a mechanism for the product owner to scope, coordinate, and prioritize the increments of user value for delivery. A user story is captured on the backlog.

User Stories represent stakeholder needs using short, simple documentation and invite exploration of the requirements through conversations, tests, and supplemental requirements representations as needed. They are concise and easy to change as stakeholder needs are better understood or as those needs evolve.

A commonly used construct for ensuring quality in user stories is the INVEST criteria, which calls for user stories to be:

- **(I) Independent**: : represents a feature which can be delivered independent of other features.

    - Example: "ATM PIN entry" is independent from 'Withdrawal Amount'

- **(N) Negotiable**: : the team can negotiate how to deliver.

- **(V) Valuable**: : expresses the value to the customer.

    - Example: "ATM PIN entry" allows only the correct person to access the account.

- **(E) Estimable**: : team can estimate effort to deliver based on past experience.

- **(S) Sized Appropriately**: : for the team to complete in one iteration. In general, the smaller the better.

- **(T) Testable**: : can be validated objectively by a stakeholder.

Not all backlog items are to be written as user stories. However, User Stories is a common technique used as they emphasize the customer value.

## 7.21.3 Elements

User Stories follow the 3Cs:

- Card,

- Conversation, and

- Confirmation.

### .1 Card

Title (optional)

The title of the user story describes an activity that the user wants to carry out with the solution. Typically, it is an active-verb goal phrase, similar to the way use cases are titled.

### .2 Format

There is no mandatory structure for user stories; however, the most popular format includes three components:

- a user role or persona [WHO],

- a necessary action, behaviour, or feature [WHAT], and

- the benefit or business value received by the user when the story is implemented [WHY].

**Example format 1**

"As a <role>, I need to <feature> so that <goal or value>."

As a current bank account holder, I need to access my account, so that I can withdraw cash.

**Example format 2**

"In order to <business value>, as a <role>, I need to <behaviour>."

In order to withdraw cash from my account, as a current bank account holder, I need access to my account.

### .3  Conversation

The intended purpose of User Stories is to communicate between stakeholders and the delivery team. The user story intentionally does not capture all there is to know about the customer need. A well-written user story invokes conversation among the team.

### .4  Confirmation

Business analysis practitioners confirm the delivered item satisfies the need expressed in the user story. This is most often expressed as acceptance criteria. Acceptance criteria define the boundaries of a user story and help verify and validate the solution met the intended user need.

Acceptance criteria help the delivery team identify the minimum amount of function necessary. Acceptance criteria are primarily used by the product owner and stakeholders to verify and validate. They also serve as a basis for acceptance tests, regression tests, exploratory tests, and other tests to be developed in support of the product.

### .5  User Story Management

There are a variety of ways in which user stories are used throughout an agile initiative. The follow techniques are all impacted by User Stories:

- 7.1 Backlog Refinement
- 7.10 Product Roadmap
- 7.18 Story Decomposition,
- 7.19 Story Elaboration, and
- 7.24 Visioning

## 7.21.4    Usage Considerations

### .1  Strengths

- Tied to small, implementable, and testable slices of functionality facilitating rapid delivery and frequent customer feedback.
- Easily understandable by stakeholders.

- Can be developed through a variety of elicitation techniques, including but not limited to facilitated workshops, contextual inquiry, and other ethnographic elicitation techniques.

- User Stories are simple enough that people can learn to write them in a few minutes, being careful about always delivering business value.

- The process of collaborating on defining and exploring stories builds team commitment and shared understanding of the business domain.

- User Stories invite conversation for further decomposition and exploration.

- To facilitate estimating, planning, and delivery, many agile teams supplement User Stories with analysis models (such as a data model, business rules, user acceptance tests, screen mock-ups or prototypes, context diagram, and state diagram).

### .2  Limitations

- This conversational approach can challenge the team, since they do not have all the answers and detailed specifications upfront.

- Too many stories can inflate the backlog.

- User Stories spawn more User Stories through decomposition, so the information must be organized to ensure it is current and relevant.

- The collection of User Stories needs to be regularly refined and prioritized.

- Teams can get too focused on individual User Stories and lose sight of the vision and product roadmap.

- This technique includes the desired feature. Teams can form habits overlooking the value statement (WHY) and instead focus on the feature (WHAT).

## 7.22          Value Modelling

### 7.22.1        Purpose

Value Modelling is used to focus solution development on value delivery by tracing decisions to the value perspective of the stakeholder.

### 7.22.2        Description

Value Modelling models value creation for stakeholders who use the solution. Value Modelling is also referred to as Customer Value Model.

Value Modelling follows a basic structure:

Customer value = Benefits – Cost

Benefits can be real (solves a problem or completes a job) or perceived (increases status, reputation, likability).

Costs include direct costs such as price and risk, and opportunity costs such as time and travel.

Value Modelling is based on a hypothesis that the purpose of an initiative is to create value for stakeholders. It works well for agile solution development, especially in large initiatives with multiple delivery teams and is a core part of user experience design.

The general steps to create a value model include:

- identifying all the stakeholders for the solution. These stakeholders can be grouped into three areas:

  - Internal and external customers.

  - Delivery team participating in the initiative.

  - Sponsor or owner providing funding.

- identifying the needs of each stakeholder group and what will provide value to each.

- identifying the process to satisfy those needs.

Value models use qualitative and quantitative research to provide structure and guidance in defining and implementing a project or initiative.

Value Modelling can be used at any Horizon:

- At the Strategy Horizon, value models focus on research and development, marketing and sales, and customers for the entire organization.

- At the Initiative and Delivery Horizons, value models focus on solution development for customers of a specific initiative.

## 7.22.3    Elements

### .1  Customer

Value Modelling focuses on delivering value to a customer; the intended customer is included in the model.

### .2  Desired Outcome or Objective

Value models capture the outcome or objective as the value to be earned or achieved by the customer.

### .3  Examples

There are several different models to portray the value model. The following examples of value models are detailed below:

- Value Proposition Canvas,

- Flow Chart of Customer Value,

- Means-Value Chart, and

- Value Model.

## .4  Value Proposition Canvas

The Value Proposition Canvas highlights the features within a product that align to the needs of the customer.

**Figure 7.22.1: Value Proposition Canvas**

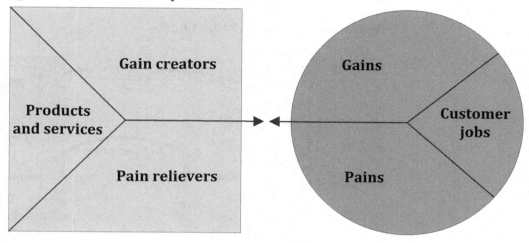

## .5  Flow Chart of Customer Value

The Flow Chart of Customer Value groups stakeholders into internal and external customers, delivery team participating, and sponsor or owner providing resources, and identifies processes to satisfy each group.

**Figure 7.22.2: Flow Chart of Customer Value**

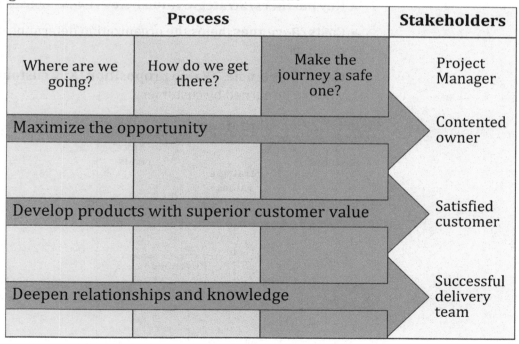

## .6 Means-Value Chart

A Means-Value Chart aligns the features or activities for stakeholders to help the customer realize value. This example uses Revenue and Profits as the central value to be realized, but it can be substituted for the organization's desired outcome.

**Figure 7.22.3: Means-Value Chart**

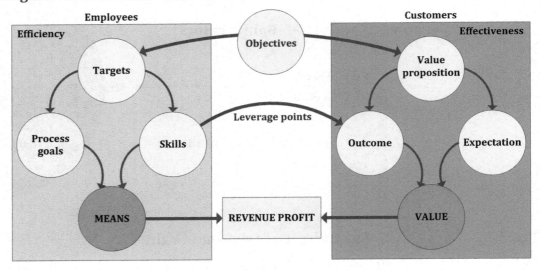

## .7 Value Model

A Value Model includes the following elements:

- **Key partners/Strategic values/Key rivals**: focuses on the people involved.

- **Costs/Revenues**: helps the organization determine if costs are less than revenue.

- **Key competencies/Value proposition/Key customers**: emphasizes the value to be earned by customers.

**Figure 7.22.4: Value Model**

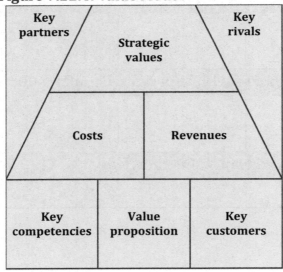

## 7.22.4      Usage Consideration

### .1   Strengths

- Can be used at any horizon.

- The structure of information is based on how the human mind works, so it documents process and shows traceability with minimal documentation.

- Structures decision making based on value created for customers and stakeholders.

### .2   Limitations

- Research makes assumptions about the stakeholders and may omit nuanced information which could change the solution or outcome.

- It can be too complicated to be advantageous to companies looking for quick information.

# 7.23      Value Stream Mapping

## 7.23.1      Purpose

Value Stream Mapping is used to provide a complete, fact-based, time-series representation of the stream of activities required to deliver a product or service to the internal or external customer.

## 7.23.2      Description

A value stream represents the flow of material and information required to bring a solution to the customer. A value stream map is a graphical representation that captures a snapshot of the value stream.

There are two main types of value stream maps that are widely used:

- **Current State Value Stream Map**: depicts a value stream as it is applied by those who are responsible for executing it. It is usually used as a starting point for analysis of an existing process to identify improvement opportunities.

- **Future State Value Stream Map**: derived from the current state and shows what the value stream will look like after the implementation of the improvements.

In an agile environment, the value stream map is usually simple and drawn on a whiteboard. It can be used to help re-engineer business processes to optimize use of software. It can also be used to re-engineer and tune the development processes, for example, to reduce lead time from solution discovery to release.

### 7.23.3     Elements

#### .1   Prepare

1. Gather a cross-functional team. In an agile context, this includes subject matter experts with business domain knowledge and technical team members such as developers, testers, operational support, architects, and vendor representatives. Business analysis practitioners frequently facilitate the session.

2. Assign a value stream map owner. Ideally, this is someone who has a deep understanding of the current process.

3. Select a product, a product family, or a service, and define the scope of the value stream map.

4. Identify the customer value received so it can be traced back.

#### .2   Create Current State

The current value stream map can be captured following these steps:

1. Name the map.

2. Observe or simulate the value stream. Follow a product or product family path by starting at the end closest to the customer and record the process working backwards to the beginning.

3. Draw the value stream map.

4. Capture the information flow that is vital for the value stream to function. Information flow includes things such as orders, schedules, inventory time, changeover time, cycle time, and the number of operators involved.

5. Build a model that shows each step in the flow with hand-offs and sequence. To assist in the analysis needed to identify opportunities for improvement in the process, ensure you include time and cost values onto the steps in the process. These time values may be estimated, if needed. The more details available, the easier it is to identify improvement opportunities.

6. Identify the waste steps to eliminate. These are steps in the flow which are redundant, low value, or could be automated.

7. Validate the value stream map. The initial draft of the current value stream map must be validated before proceeding to the improvement phase.

### .3  Analyze Current State

The current value stream map can be analyzed as described in the *BABOK® Guide* technique Root Cause Analysis to identify value added steps (such as transformation processes) from those that are non-value added, such as excessive inventories (for more information see *BABOK® Guide*: 10.40 Root Cause Analysis).

The non-value added steps can be analyzed further to determine which ones are necessary (such as meeting regulatory requirements) and which ones are unnecessary (such as excessive paperwork).

### .4  Create Future State

The future state value stream map can be drawn as follows:

1. Identify improvement areas. Unnecessary non-value added steps are the source of waste and they can be eliminated. Team members can mark these areas (such as reducing lead time) on the current value stream map.

2. Identify improvement measurements.

3. Capture the future state value stream map. Draw the value stream map that shows what the value stream will look like after you have eliminated the waste (unnecessary wait time, excessive administrative paperwork, high inventories, and so forth).

4. Once the future state is captured it can be used as the target state of the improvement initiative.

### .5  Implement Process Improvement

1. Identify supporting material required for implementing the improvement such as information technology systems, training, and changeover.

2. Implement the improvement.

In an agile context, Value Stream Mapping is frequently used when implementing process improvement. Often, the changes to be made in the business process will require changes to or implementation of supporting technology products. The requirements for these changes or enhancements become backlog items that feed into an agile initiative.

Once the improvement is made, the future state becomes the current value stream map and it can be used as a starting point for another improvement cycle.

The following is an example of a value stream map.

**Figure 7.23.1: Value Stream Map**

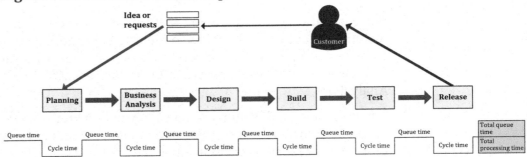

### 7.23.4    Usage Considerations

#### .1  Strengths

- More comprehensive than a process flow diagram.
- Provides a blueprint for implementing improvement.
- Establishes a shared understanding of process waste and bottlenecks.
- Provides a common visual language for diverse stakeholders.

#### .2  Limitations

- Not easy to construct in comparison with other visual modelling techniques.
- Can look daunting because of all the information captured.
- Mapping paralysis. It is easy to get caught making the current state value stream map complete and perfect instead of proceeding to the improvement stage.
- Doesn't work well in knowledge based or non-linear work.
- Leads to disruptive or "re-engineering" approach. Doesn't work well with ongoing improvement efforts.

## 7.24    Visioning

### 7.24.1    Purpose

Visioning is used to determine the desired outcome for an initiative worded in a concise and approachable manner.

**7.24.2**  **Description**

The purpose of an initiative is to deliver value towards an organization's business goal. Visioning creates aspirational guidance that is used to understand if efforts align to desired outcomes and add value. Visioning facilitates a shared understanding of the strategy for the organization or initiative. Visioning allows the team to orient all work towards the vision.

An initiative achieves value when it delivers value that contributes to an organization's business goals, for example

- increasing or protecting revenue,
- creating a new opportunity,
- reducing or avoiding costs,
- reducing or avoiding risks,
- meeting regulatory obligations,
- improving customer experience and brand awareness,
- implementing a marketing strategy, or
- developing staff.

Examples of good vision statements include:

- NASA vision: Put a man on the moon.
- Apple iPod vision: All your music in one place in your pocket.
- Renovate my kitchen using the same layout but modern finishes and style.
- Increase application completion and shorten time for completion through the web experience.

**7.24.3**  **Elements**

**.1  Vision Statement**

Business value is to be expressed as a range or set of benefits. The evolution of clarity about business value increases understanding of why a solution is needed. An important aspect of expressing business value is the conversation that generates the shared understanding.

The vision consists of a simple statement represented visually with images or words which conveys the goal and scope for the initiative.

### .2 Vision Exercise

Business analysis practitioners facilitate a vision exercise session with key stakeholders to determine the vision statement. Exercises such as Product Box and Product Differentiation Statement can be particularly useful.

### .3 Impact Metrics

This is specific information which can be measured objectively and will indicate whether the organization is achieving the vision for the initiative. These are often correlating metrics, not causation metrics.

## 7.24.4 Usage Consideration

### .1 Strengths

- Specifies what is considered in and what is out for the product or initiative.
- Focuses the team and stakeholders on the organizational value to be achieved.
- Helps the organization decide when enough product is delivered to stop working on this initiative.

### .2 Limitations

- Teams may treat Visioning as a check-the-box activity by initially facilitating and identifying good information, but fail to reference or refine later based on feedback and learning.
- The visioning effort provides no value if the team does not use the information for decision making and prioritization.
- While Visioning can align and motivate people, it can also lead to confirmation bias if people attach to one solution and fail to learn from evidence.
- The best Visioning depends on the imagination, diversity, trust, and ability to collaborate in the group. Otherwise, the vision can lead the team to make wrong decisions.
- Visioning can lead to people narrowing focus to one solution instead of exploring many options.

# Appendix A: Glossary

## a

acceptance criteria: Criteria associated with requirements, products, or the delivery cycle that must be met in order to achieve stakeholder acceptance.

acceptance test driven development: Occurs when team members with different perspectives (customer, development, testing) collaborate to identify acceptance criteria and subsequent tests in advance of implementing the corresponding functionality. These acceptance tests represent the user's point of view and act as a form of requirements to describe how the system will function, as well as serve as a way of verifying that the system functions as intended. In some cases the team automates the acceptance tests.

adaptive planning: An approach to planning where long-term plans are constantly reviewed and revised to account for new information learned during the course of a project.

agile manifesto: A statement of the values that underpin Agile Software Development. It was drafted from February 11th through 13th, 2001.

anti-pattern: A commonly used, yet ineffective, process or practice.

assumption: An influencing factor that is believed to be true but has not been confirmed to be accurate, or that could be true now but may not be in the future.

ATDD: see *acceptance test driven development*.

## b

backlog: An ordered list of options that represent changes to a solution. Various frameworks use backlogs to represent the changes for a given scope.

backlog item: An element on a backlog that represents a potential change to a product. Backlog items can take the form of user stories, spikes, defects, infrastructure work, refactors, documents or other item types that a team finds useful in their context.

BDD: See *behaviour driven development*.

business domain: See *Domain*.

business goal: A state or condition that an organization is seeking to establish and maintain, usually expressed qualitatively rather than quantitatively.

business objective: An objective, measurable result to indicate that a business goal has been achieved.

business rules: A specific, practicable, testable directive that is under the control of the business and that serves as a criterion for guiding behaviour, shaping judgments, or making decisions.

business value: In management, business value is an informal term that includes all forms of value that determine the health and well-being of the firm in the long run. In agile development, an output delivers business value when it increases or protects revenue or reduces or avoids costs for an organization.

# c

change: The act of transformation in response to a need.

collaboration: The act of two or more people working together towards a common goal.

constraint: An influencing factor that cannot be changed, and that places a limit or restriction on a possible solution or solution option.

context: The circumstances that influence, are influenced by, and provide understanding of the change.

context diagram: The highest level data flow diagram which represents the system in its entirety, as the area under study with external organizations, people, or systems as the source or target of data flows.

core concept model (business analysis): One of six ideas that are fundamental to the practice of business analysis: Change, Need, Solution, Context, Stakeholder, and Value.

customer: A stakeholder who uses or may use products or services produced by the enterprise and may have contractual or moral rights that the enterprise is obliged to meet.

customer representative: an individual who works with the team to represent the perspective of stakeholders who use or may use products or services produced by the enterprise and may have contractual or moral rights that the enterprise is obliged to meet.

# d

data model: A diagram that describes the entities, classes or data objects relevant to a domain, the attributes that are used to describe them, and the relationships among them to provide a common set of semantics for analysis and implementation.

decision maker: Person or people responsible for making the final decision.

definition of done: A technique where the team agrees on, and prominently displays, a list of criteria which must be met before a backlog item is considered done.

definition of ready: A technique where the team agrees on, and prominently displays, a list of criteria which must be met before a backlog item is considered ready for the team to start delivery work.

**delivery team:** A cross-functional team of skilled individuals who bring a variety of expertise to bear on the process of building a software product.

**design:** A usable representation of a solution.

**domain:** The sphere of knowledge that defines a set of common requirements, terminology, and functionality for any program or initiative solving a problem.

**done:** See *Definition of Done.*

## e

**elicitation:** Iterative derivation and extraction of information from stakeholders or other sources.

**ethnographic elicitation techniques:** Iterative derivation and extraction of information from stakeholders or other sources by observing users in their work environment and looking at business processes from the perspective of the user.

**examples:** An approach to defining the behaviour of a system using realistic examples instead of abstract statements. Examples are often used to further describe user stories and are used both as guidance for development and testing.

**experiments:** Elicitation performed in a controlled manner to make a discovery, test a hypothesis, or demonstrate a known fact.

## f

**feature:** A distinguishing characteristic of a solution that implements a cohesive set of requirements and which delivers value for a set of stakeholders.

**fibonacci scale:** A scale commonly used when sizing user stories that is based on the Fibonacci Sequence – a series of numbers characterized by the fact that every number after the first two is the sum of the two preceding ones. In practice teams use a modified sequence that stops the pattern at larger numbers. Generally, the scale includes the following numbers: 0, 1, 2, 3, 5, 8,13.

**framework:** A collection of specific practices and ideas that have been proven useful in a specific context that teams can use as a basis to create their own methodology.

## g

**goal:** See *business goal.*

# h

**horizon** A view of work within an organization with a level of granularity appropriate to the time frame being planned for and the nature of the feedback loops used.

# i

**initiative:** A specific project, program, or action taken to solve some business problem(s) or achieve some specific change objective(s).

**information radiator:** A handwritten, drawn, printed, or electronic display which a team places in a highly visible location, so that all team members as well as passers-by can see the latest information about their work at a glance.

**iteration:** A defined time period when increments of a product are developed and tested and made ready to deliver to the customer.

**iterative planning:** An approach to planning that intentionally allows for repeating planning activities, and for potentially revisiting the same plan to update it based on new information. These planning activities are repeated in some agile approaches in regular iterations or time-boxes.

# m

**methodology:** A body of methods, techniques, procedures, working concepts, and rules used to solve a problem.

**metric:** A quantifiable level of an indicator measured at a specified point in time.

**minimal marketable feature:** A small, self-contained feature that can be developed quickly and delivers significant value to the user.

**minimum viable product:** A concept from Lean Startup that describes the fastest way to get through the Build-Measure-Learn feedback loop with the minimum amount of effort.

**model:** A representation and simplification of reality developed to convey information to a specific audience to support analysis, communication, and understanding.

**monitoring:** Collecting data on a continuous basis from a solution in order to determine how well a solution is implemented compared to expected results.

**MMF:** See *minimal marketable feature*.

**MVP:** See *minimum viable product*.

# n

need A problem or opportunity to be addressed.

# o

objective: See *business objective*.

outcome: The change in the organization and changes in the behaviour of stakeholders as a result of an initiative.

output: Anything that your team delivers as part of your initiative. This includes software, documentation, processes, and other things that tend to be measured in order to gauge how the initiative is going.

# p

persona: Fictional characters or archetypes that exemplify the way that typical users will interact with a product.

planning horizon: See *Horizon*.

predictive planning: An approach to planning that involves detailed analysis and planning at the beginning of the project for the duration of the project and then acting on that plan. Predictive planning is based on the assumption that the later a mistake is found, the more it will cost to fix it. This results in the desire to plan the entire project at the beginning of the project and avoid changes to the plan as much as possible.

product (business analysis): A solution or component of a solution that is the result of an initiative.

product box: A collaboration framework where a team and customers design a box for their product in order to determine the characteristics of a product that customers want to buy.

product differentiation statement: An expression of how a given product fills a particular consumer need in a way that its competitors don't.

product owner: The role on the team that represents the interests of all stakeholders, defines the features of the product, and prioritizes the product backlog.

product roadmap: A visual representation of how a team plans to implement their product strategy over progressively longer time horizons. The product roadmap is updated frequently, and reflects outcomes the team plans to realize rather than outputs the team plans to deliver.

progressive elaboration: The act of continually defining requirements with successively greater levels of detail as needed through the life of the product or the feature within a product.

**r**

relative estimation: A way of estimating work effort by identifying features/requirements with stories and then assigning story points to stories. The cumulative story points represent the estimated amount of effort required to deliver the story. The story points are then calculated against the team's velocity to create an estimate on how much the team can deliver in a particular iteration.

release planning: At the beginning of a project the team will create a high-level release plan. The team cannot possibly know everything upfront so a detailed plan is not necessary. The release plan should address:

- the number and duration of the iterations,

- how many people or teams should be on this project,

- the number of releases, the value delivered in each release, and

- the ship date for the releases.

requirement: A usable representation of a need.

retrospective: Retrospectives are a variation of project retrospectives whereby the retrospective workshop is conducted at regular intervals throughout the delivery process, such as after each iteration and/or release.

rolling planning: Rolling planning is a technique whereby a team plans for an iteration for only the time period where they have reasonable certainty. As that time comes to an end the team plans out for another time period, determined by their level of certainty.

risk: The effect of uncertainty on the value of a change, a solution, or the enterprise. See also residual risk.

**s**

service level agreements: Formal agreements that contract level of service and performance.

solution: A specific way of satisfying one or more needs in a context.

stakeholder: A group or individual with a relationship to the change, the need, or the solution.

state diagram: An analysis model showing the life cycle of a data entity or class.

**story mapping:** A technique to facilitate the understanding of product functionality, the flow of usage, and to assist with prioritizing product delivery (such as release planning). The output of the story mapping exercise is a product called a story map, which describes a workflow of user stories. Story maps may break down user stories into tasks for each process and may represent these tasks based on priority.

## t

**three amigos session:** A gathering of the people with three primary perspectives to examine an increment of work before, during, and after development. Those perspectives are:

- Business – What problem are we trying to solve?

- Development – How might we build a solution to solve that problem?

- Testing – What about this, what could possibly happen?

**time-box:** An agreed upon period of time in which an activity is conducted or a defined deliverable is intended to be produced.

## u

**user story:** A small, concise statement of functionality or quality needed to deliver value to a specific stakeholder.

**user story mapping:** See *story mapping*.

## v

**value (business analysis):** The worth, importance, or usefulness of something to a stakeholder in a context.

**value stream mapping:** A complete, fact-based, time-series representation of the stream of activities required to deliver a product or service.

## w

**wireframes:** A two-dimensional illustration of a user interface that focuses on space allocation and prioritization of content, functionalities available, and intended behaviours. Wireframes typically do not include any styling, color, or graphics.

# Appendix B: Mapping BABOK Guide Tasks to Horizons

The following table demonstrates how each BABOK® Guide task can be applied with an agile mindset at each horizon.

This mapping is provided for general guidance and reference purposes and does not preclude the creative application of any task at any horizon.

| BABOK Guide Knowledge Area | BABOK Guide Tasks | How Task Applies at the Strategy Horizon | How Task Applies at the Initiative Horizon | How Task Applies at the Delivery Horizon |
|---|---|---|---|---|
| 3. Business Analysis Planning and Monitoring | 3.1 Plan Business Analysis Approach | This first step in planning the business analysis approach is making the determination that agile will be used as the approach. The level of planning is lightweight and just what is needed to meet the needs of the horizon.<br><br>The agile approach is continually redefined and business analysis methods change and evolve as feedback is received. | The specific agile business analysis approaches and activities are selected at the Initiative Horizon. The level of planning is lightweight and just what is needed to meet the needs of the horizon.<br><br>The agile approaches and activities are continually redefined and business analysis methods change and evolve as feedback is received. | At the Delivery Horizon, the team plans the best way – most rapid, efficient, or accurate – to decompose features to stories for the immediate work effort, and in alignment with the team priorities and context.<br><br>The agile approaches and activities are continually redefined and business analysis methods change and evolve as feedback is received. |
| | 3.2 Plan Stakeholder Engagement | The plans for stakeholder engagement are relative to the specific needs of the Strategy Horizon.<br><br>The approach for establishing and maintaining effective working relationships with the stakeholders is an ongoing adaptive process and includes stakeholders from across all initiatives in the organization who have a longer view of the organizational goals and strategy. | The plans for stakeholder engagement are relative to the specific needs of the Initiative Horizon.<br><br>The approach for establishing and maintaining effective working relationships with the stakeholders is an ongoing adaptive process and includes stakeholders from across all initiatives in the organization who are responsible for executing on organizational goals. | The plans for stakeholder engagement are relative to the specific needs of the Delivery Horizon.<br><br>The approach for establishing and maintaining effective working relationships with the stakeholders is an ongoing adaptive process and includes stakeholders from across all initiatives in the organization who have direct interaction with the solution and provide in-depth and detailed feedback regarding the solution. |

| BABOK Guide Knowledge Area | BABOK Guide Tasks | How Task Applies at the Strategy Horizon | How Task Applies at the Initiative Horizon | How Task Applies at the Delivery Horizon |
|---|---|---|---|---|
| | 3.3 Plan Business Analysis Governance | Define how decisions are made about requirements and designs, including reviews, change control, approvals, and prioritization. Involves establishing a portfolio management approach and a decision framework for the entire organization. Governance and decision frameworks are adaptive based on the evolving understanding of relative risk across the organization. | Define how management of the initiative requirements will take place. This includes determining if Scrum, Kanban, or another agile approach will be used. The team determines how the backlog will be refined and prioritized throughout the initiative. | The delivery team defines what business analysis governance is needed to define decisions for requirements. This includes how refinement will happen, what information radiators are needed for stakeholders, and how changes will be communicated within the team. |
| | 3.4 Plan Business Analysis Information Management | The approach for how business analysis information will be stored and accessed is defined through ongoing collaboration with all initiatives across the organization to ensure consistent processes. To facilitate continuous improvements, feedback and learning is shared with the other horizons. | The approach for how business analysis information will be stored and accessed is defined through ongoing collaboration with the delivery teams involved in the initiative. To facilitate continuous improvements, feedback and learning is shared with the other horizons. | The approach for how business analysis information will be stored and accessed is defined through ongoing collaboration within the delivery team. To facilitate continuous improvements, feedback and learning is shared with the other horizons. |

| BABOK Guide Knowledge Area | BABOK Guide Tasks | How Task Applies at the Strategy Horizon | How Task Applies at the Initiative Horizon | How Task Applies at the Delivery Horizon |
|---|---|---|---|---|
| | 3.5 Identify Business Analysis Performance Improvements | Assessing business analysis work and planning to improve processes is continuous and based on ongoing feedback. Measures focus on the ability to learn and adapt based on ongoing feedback. | Assessing business analysis work and planning to improve processes is continuous and based on ongoing feedback. Measures focus on the ability to learn and adapt based on ongoing feedback | Business analysis practitioners consider improvements that can be made to ongoing analysis activities. Speed and accuracy become very important in analysis practiced at the Delivery Horizon, and any process improvements that are identified are considered for implementation. Assessing business analysis work and planning to improve processes is continuous and based on ongoing feedback. Measures focus on the ability to learn and adapt based on ongoing feedback. |
| 4. Elicitation and Collaboration | 4.1 Prepare for Elicitation | Preparing for elicitation involves creating and supporting a framework for collaboration and learning across all initiatives and using feedback to ensure continuous improvement in elicitation outcomes. | Preparing for elicitation involves creating and supporting a framework for collaboration and learning across all delivery teams and using feedback to ensure continuous improvement in elicitation outcomes. | Preparing for elicitation considers what kinds of elicitation are necessary: decomposing features to stories? Reviewing stories? Elaborating on features already underway? Each may require different preparation. |

| BABOK Guide Knowledge Area | BABOK Guide Tasks | How Task Applies at the Strategy Horizon | How Task Applies at the Initiative Horizon | How Task Applies at the Delivery Horizon |
|---|---|---|---|---|
| | 4.2 Conduct Elicitation | The focus of conducting elicitation is continuous and spans across all initiatives, throughout the organization, and spans beyond the boundaries of the organization. The focus is on ensuring that ongoing feedback is heard, and that ongoing organizational learning extends across all initiatives | The focus when conducting elicitation is to identify information that allows features to be broken down into stories. This information is also used to determine the order and priorities of delivering those features. | Conducting elicitation may take different forms at the Delivery Horizon. Communication may be casual or formal, consistent or sporadic, but it is always continuous. |
| | 4.3 Confirm Elicitation Results | Confirming elicitation results involves ensuring that feedback is both consistent and still relevant. At the Strategy Horizon, decisions can be based on both what is likely to be true and what is actually true. It is important to communicate a clear understanding on which elicitation results are assumptions and which are facts. | Confirming elicitation results involves ensuring that feedback received from all horizons is both consistent and still relevant. Confirmation occurs from feedback from other horizons | Confirming elicitation results may be specific to reviewing a discussion or communication, but may also be done as the review and approval of user stories for implementation |

| BABOK Guide Knowledge Area | BABOK Guide Tasks | How Task Applies at the Strategy Horizon | How Task Applies at the Initiative Horizon | How Task Applies at the Delivery Horizon |
|---|---|---|---|---|
| | 4.4 Communicate Business Analysis Information | Ensuring stakeholders have a shared understanding of business analysis information involves establishing and actively supporting an environment for constructive communication, collaboration, and continuous improvement throughout the organization. This can be done through visioning, the product roadmap, and story maps | At the Initiative Horizon, the emphasis is on communicating information to stakeholders and collecting feedback and information from customers. This can be done through reviews, product demonstrations, workshops, release plans, and the product roadmap. | At the Delivery Horizon, communicating business analysis information includes communicating cross-team dependencies and discussing priorities with stakeholders. Context and analysis models help communicate how backlog items align to the desired outcome. |
| | 4.5 Manage Stakeholder Collaboration | Encouraging stakeholders to work towards a common goal involves establishing an environment for constructive communication, collaboration, and continuous improvement throughout the organization | Driving collaboration and connection is a core agile value, and a core agile business analysis value. Find ways to ensure that your activities are transparent and communicated. | Driving collaboration and connection is a core agile value, and a core agile business analysis value. Business analysis practitioners find ways to ensure that activities are transparent and communicated. |

| BABOK Guide Knowledge Area | BABOK Guide Tasks | How Task Applies at the Strategy Horizon | How Task Applies at the Initiative Horizon | How Task Applies at the Delivery Horizon |
|---|---|---|---|---|
| 5. Requirements Life Cycle Management | 5.1 Trace Requirements | Tracing requirements at the Strategy Horizon involves determining if the changes in one initiative impact any other initiatives in the organization. Efforts focus on ensuring initiatives contribute to business goals and measuring impact. Effective implementation at this level limits work in progress to shorten the delivery cycle. Requirements may be ambiguous and focus on organizational goals. Ensure feedback frameworks are in place to support the ongoing alignment to evolving organizational goals. | Efforts focus on ensuring requirements are traceable to the business goals and metrics established in the Strategy Horizon. Effective requirements tracing ensures efforts within one initiative are aligned to and not in conflict with other initiatives within the organization. | Stories are traced to features, which may in turn be traced to the desired outcomes. Additional tracings may be made to business goals, users affected, and any number of metrics. Efforts focus on aligning backlog items and requirements to the product roadmap and goals. |

| BABOK Guide Knowledge Area | BABOK Guide Tasks | How Task Applies at the Strategy Horizon | How Task Applies at the Initiative Horizon | How Task Applies at the Delivery Horizon |
|---|---|---|---|---|
| | 5.2 Maintain Requirements | Maintaining requirements is focused less on maintaining accurate requirements and more on understanding the accuracy of customer needs and lessons from customer experience, and determining if existing information remains relevant. This may involve a trade-off between accurate maintenance of requirements in favour of experimentation, continual change, and learning. | Maintaining requirements is focused less on maintaining accurate requirements and more on understanding the accuracy of customer needs and lessons from customer experience, and determining if existing information remains relevant. This may involve a trade-off between accurate maintenance of requirements in favour of experimentation, continual change, and learning. The focus is on the selection of which features to deliver, not necessarily the order in which they are delivered. | User stories and features are monitored for staleness. As time passes, it is likely that the business need, business environment, technical environment, or customer need will have changed. User stories may need to be revised, re-prioritized, or removed. |
| | 5.3 Prioritize Requirements | Prioritize Requirements focuses on the prioritization of organizational goals and initiatives rather than detailed requirements. Feedback and learning from inside and outside the organization is central to understanding what and how to prioritize goals and initiatives. | At the Initiative Horizon, the focus is on the selection of which features to deliver, not necessarily the order in which they are delivered. | At the Delivery Horizon there is frequent change to the prioritization of backlog items as learning occurs from delivered stories and completed features. |

| BABOK Guide Knowledge Area | BABOK Guide Tasks | How Task Applies at the Strategy Horizon | How Task Applies at the Initiative Horizon | How Task Applies at the Delivery Horizon |
|---|---|---|---|---|
| | 5.4 Assess Requirements Changes | Evaluating the implications of proposed changes to requirements and designs, the Strategy Horizon focuses on understanding how changes impact organizational goals and impact changes that extend beyond initiatives. Assessments are based on continuous feedback and learning | Requirement changes are assessed during backlog refinement activities. This is a lightweight activity and only done on an as-needed basis | User stories and features are monitored for staleness. As time passes, it is likely that the business need, business environment, technical environment, or customer need will have changed. User stories may need to be revised, re-prioritized, or removed. |
| | 5.5 Approve Requirements | At the Strategy Horizon, approving requirements involves empowering initiatives to understand what is doable through ongoing communication of evolving assumptions, constraints, and goals. | Agile initiatives generally appoint a lead such as a product owner or customer representative. Approval happens when the lead selects a requirement for delivery. Reducing the number of approvals needed can help ensure that the team can deliver quickly and focus on increasing feedback and learning opportunities. | The creator of an artifact or deliverable has their work approved by someone other than themselves, preferably someone with a view of the desired value being delivered. User stories and any supporting documents are frequently approved by the business owner in this task. |
| 6. Strategy Analysis | 6.1 Analyze Current State | Analyzing the current state is done through collaboration, continuous feedback, and learning. As the current state evolves, it is continuously re-analyzed to understand the impact of the change. | When beginning an initiative, business analysis practitioners analyze the current state. Analysis focuses on understanding the whole at a high-level and then identifying the most valuable parts for change. | Collaborating with the product owner and others, business analysis practitioners examine a specific portion of the current solution. Care is given to keep scope focused on those things that will be immediately affected, given the nature of the Delivery Horizon. |

| BABOK Guide Knowledge Area | BABOK Guide Tasks | How Task Applies at the Strategy Horizon | How Task Applies at the Initiative Horizon | How Task Applies at the Delivery Horizon |
|---|---|---|---|---|
| | 6.2 Define Future State | Defining the future state is done through collaboration, continuous feedback, and learning. As the future state evolves, it is continuously re-analyzed to understand the impact of the change.<br><br>Multiple potential future states and different time horizons are continually being defined and re-defined while change is happening. | At the Initiative Horizon, defining the future state involves identifying the intended outcome of the initiative.<br><br>Multiple potential future states and different time horizons are continually being defined and re-defined while change is happening. | The immediate future state is considered and defined, focusing on the value that will be delivered in the upcoming delivery cycle. Current work is assessed to ensure it aligns to the desired outcomes of the initiative. |
| | 6.3 Assess Risks | Assessing both positive and negative risk is ongoing for multiple potential future states and different time frames.<br><br>Assumptions and hypotheses around risks associated with the evolving multiple future states are continually explored and understood as a means of ongoing risk mitigation. | The ongoing assessment of risk, based on continuous feedback and learning, helps determine which features to work on first. | Business analysis practitioners consider what could go well, poorly, and what could influence the work and the value being delivered. |

| BABOK Guide Knowledge Area | BABOK Guide Tasks | How Task Applies at the Strategy Horizon | How Task Applies at the Initiative Horizon | How Task Applies at the Delivery Horizon |
|---|---|---|---|---|
| | 6.4 Define Change Strategy | At the Strategy Horizon, the change strategy is defined with the focus of aligning initiatives to organizational goals. This includes impact goals or metrics to measure whether an initiative positively influences the strategy. | Continuous feedback and learning informs an ever evolving change strategy. Multiple potential strategies may be defined through experimentation. | Change strategy is lightweight and is done at the completion of each delivery release. When a set of requirements for a product or service is released to stakeholders, the team elicits feedback to understand if the requirements met the need and solved the problem. Based on this feedback, the team can make any necessary changes to the backlog. |
| 7. Requirements Analysis and Design Definition | 7.1 Specify and Model Requirements | The Strategy Horizon specifies and models the goals of the organization. | The Initiative Horizon specifies and models stakeholder needs and problems to be solved. | The Delivery Horizon specifies and models requirements in the form of lightweight documentation such as user stories, job stories, wireframes, or product backlog items. |
| | 7.2 Verify Requirements | The Strategy Horizon ensures that the initiatives are meeting the goals of the organization. | Verifying requirements involves communicating a shared understanding of the problem and the solution. This facilitates a shared understanding of the features and ensures the delivery team can act on them. | Requirements meet quality needed if the delivery team can clearly understand, collaborate to deliver, and validate requirements. Verifying is a lightweight activity that demonstrates team agreement. |
| | 7.3 Validate Requirements | The Strategy Horizon ensures that the initiatives are aligned to the goals of the organization | The ongoing validation of outputs based on continuous feedback and learning helps the evolution towards the desired outcomes of the initiative. | All requirements are validated against the need with the solution is delivered. This can be automated through Behaviour Driven Development or manual through user acceptance testing |

| BABOK Guide Knowledge Area | BABOK Guide Tasks | How Task Applies at the Strategy Horizon | How Task Applies at the Initiative Horizon | How Task Applies at the Delivery Horizon |
|---|---|---|---|---|
| | 7.4 Define Requirements Architecture | The Strategy Horizon ensures that the initiatives are aligned to the goals of the organization. | Requirements architecture is managed through the backlog. Techniques such as Purpose Alignment Model, Retrospectives, and Value Stream Mapping are used on an ongoing basis to ensure feedback and learning informs the evolution of the requirements architecture. | Business analysis practitioners collaborate with the delivery team to decide on the form of user stories as well as what other supporting artifacts will be used. Requirements may include necessary metadata such as traceability to features, metrics, and other sources. |
| | 7.5 Define Design Options | While the detailed design options are defined elsewhere, the vision for the customer journey and high-level user experience can be defined at the Strategy Horizon. | Design options are continually being defined and redefined based on ongoing feedback and learning. Multiple design options may be investigated through experimentation as a means to determine which option to pursue. | Design options are evaluated and selected, collaboratively and with input from team members and stakeholders. A user story narrative form will frequently leave the greatest possible room for the design to fulfill the requirements. The actual form of those may be decided on or altered at the last responsible moment, which may be within the time frame of the Delivery Horizon. |
| | 7.6 Analyze Potential Value and Recommend Solution | The scope of analysis is do just enough analysis to decide to start an initiative or not. Ensuring continuous collaboration and feedback between initiatives aids this analysis. The strategy for the vision of creating value is defined at the Strategy Horizon. | Experimentation is used to analyze potential value and make solution recommendations. | Collaboration, feedback, and learning are used to select solution options or make decisions with key stakeholders such as the product owner. |

| BABOK Guide Knowledge Area | BABOK Guide Tasks | How Task Applies at the Strategy Horizon | How Task Applies at the Initiative Horizon | How Task Applies at the Delivery Horizon |
|---|---|---|---|---|
| 8. Solution Evaluation | 8.1 Measure Solution Performance | Measuring a solution's performance involves measuring the feedback from all initiatives to determine if organizational goals are being achieved. | Solution performance is measured based on a continual assessment of outcomes achieved. Ongoing learning and feedback from metrics with quick time frames provide indicators that the desired outcomes are on target. | Implemented stories should be altering solution performance, either individually or as they accumulate. Stories have the expectation that they will move one or more metrics in a known direction. That expectation may or may not be fulfilled; this becomes an important source of learning and feedback. |
| | 8.2 Analyze Performance Measures | Analyzing performance measures focuses on assessing the holistic value provided by all initiatives across the organization | Analyzing performance is measured through a continual assessment of outcomes achieved. Ongoing learning and feedback from metrics with quick time frames provide indicators that the desired outcomes are on target. | Analyzing performance measures at the Delivery Horizon will help inform the decision of whether to continue, discontinue, or change the stories currently in the backlog. For example, once sufficient beneficial change has been achieved that is related to a particular feature, the team may choose to work on a different feature. |
| | 8.3 Assess Solution Limitations | At the Strategy Horizon, assessing solution limitations involves collaboration and communicating solution limitations across all initiatives. The feasibility of strategic options and value trade-offs are assessed | Solution limitations are assessed through ongoing feedback and learning throughout the initiative. Unintended consequences are frequently discovered. | The purpose is to identify any limitations that would affect the delivery options. For example, a team should identify any infrastructure limitations to the intended solution.<br><br>This is lightweight and focusing on what is known now and what is needed now for delivery. |

| BABOK Guide Knowledge Area | BABOK Guide Tasks | How Task Applies at the Strategy Horizon | How Task Applies at the Initiative Horizon | How Task Applies at the Delivery Horizon |
|---|---|---|---|---|
| | 8.4 Assess Enterprise Limitations | Assessing enterprise limitations involves continually understanding and communicating limitations to the realization of value across initiatives as these limitations evolve along with the solution. | The ongoing assessment of enterprise limitations define the constraints that impact solution design. | This task is not completed in the Delivery Horizon. |
| | 8.5 Recommend Actions to Increase Solution Value | The Strategy Horizon is responsible for recommending changes to goals or strategy. This includes recommending to start, stop, or change an initiative. Recommended changes are based on ongoing feedback and learning. | The Initiative Horizon is responsible for recommending changes to the outcomes of the initiative. This includes recommending to start, stop, or change an initiative. Recommended changes are based on ongoing feedback and learning. | This activity is of high priority at the Delivery Horizon. A subtle difference in implemented stories is where value can be enhanced or diminished. Learning and feedback about implementations and metrics will drive this activity. |

# Appendix C: Contributors

## C.1      Core Team of Authors

IIBA® and The Agile Alliance® would like to thank the following contributors to the *Agile Extension to the BABOK® Guide.* Without their efforts and commitment, the *Agile Extension to the BABOK® Guide* version 2.0 would not be possible.

- James King
- Jas Phul, Product Owner, IIBA
- Kent J. McDonald
- Paul Stapleton, Editor, IIBA
- Ryland Leyton
- Shane Hastie, Team Facilitator, The Agile Alliance
- Stephanie Vineyard
- Steve Adolph

## C.2      Expert Advisory and Review Group

The following industry experts generously provided IIBA® and The Agile Alliance® with advice and guidance on the scope and content of version 2.0 of the *Agile Extension to the BABOK® Guide* during its planning and development, and helped to shape the content and direction of this release.

- Ellan Young
- Linda Cook
- Angela Wick
- Mary Gorman
- Chirs Matts
- Ali Mazer
- Luiz Claudio Parzianello
- Zoya Royblat
- Tim Coventry
- Mindy Bohannon
- Ellen Gottesdiener

## C.3     Agile Extension to the BABOK ® Guide version 1 Contributors

- Ali Mazer
- Brian Hemker
- Carol Scalice
- Chris Matts
- David C. Cook
- David Morris
- Dennis Stevens
- Ellen Gottesdiener
- Kevin Brennan
- Luiz Claudio Parzianello
- Marsha Hughes
- Pascal Van Cauwenberghe
- Paul Stapleton, Editor
- Peter Gordon
- Shane Hastie
- Steve Erlank
- Susan Block

## C.4     Other Significant Contributors

- Irena Duniskvaric: Technical illustrations
- Lynda Sydney, Ignite Writing Services: Copy editing
- Vic Bhai, Technical Writer/Editor, IIBA: Layout and design

# Appendix D: Summary of Changes from Agile Extension to the BABOK® Guide version 1

The *Agile Extension to the BABOK® Guide* (*Agile Extension*) has be entirely re-thought and re-architected for version 2. There is no direct mapping of changes for *Agile Extension* version 1 to *Agile Extension* version 2. This appendix provides details into the rational for the changes and results of these changes.

The Agile Extension to the *BABOK® Guide* (Agile Extension) version 2 describes the benefits, activities, tasks, skills, and practices required for effective agile business analysis with a constant focus on delivering business value.

The *Agile Extension* version 2:

- positions agile business analysis beyond software development. The thinking and practices found in *Agile Extension* version 2 can be applied in any domain operating in an agile context.

- places a increased focus on agile business analysis practices and thinking as a means to helping business analysis practitioners and organizations realize the value delivered by effective agile business analysis.

- embraces and incorporates the

- *Business Analysis Core Concept Model™* (*BACCM™*).

- builds on values established in the Manifesto for Agile Software Development by describing and ingraining the seven principles for agile business analysis.

- introduces the concept of rolling planning horizons that, from an agile perspective, represent a view of work within an organization with a level of granularity appropriate to the planning time frame and the nature of the feedback loops.

- places increased emphasis on the importance of feedback and learning to the continuous delivery of value.

- rethinks, updates, adds, and removes techniques that support agile business analysis practices. Some techniques found in

*Agile Extension* version 1 have be included in *BABOK® Guide*. Unless there is a significant difference to the technique in an agile context, these techniques are not included in the *Agile Extension* version 2..

| Agile Extension version 1 Technique | Agile Extension version 2 Technique | Change |
|---|---|---|
| Backlog Management | | Moved to *BABOK® Guide* |
| | Backlog Refinement | New |
| Behaviour Driven Development | Behaviour Driven Development | Updated |
| Business Capability Analysis | | Moved to *BABOK® Guide* |
| Business Value Definition | | Removed |
| Collaborative Games | | Moved to *BABOK® Guide* |
| | Impact Mapping | New |
| | Job Stories | New |
| Kano Analysis | Kano Analysis | Updated |
| Lightweight Documentation | | Removed |
| MoSCoW Prioritization | | Removed |
| | Minimal Viable Product | New |
| Personas | Personas | Updated |
| Planning Workshop | Planning Workshop | Updated |
| | Portfolio Kanban | New |
| | Product Roadmap | New |
| Purpose Alignment Model | Purpose Alignment Model | Updated |
| Real Options | Real Options | Updated |
| Relative Estimation | Relative Estimation | Updated |
| Retrospectives | Retrospectives | Updated |
| | Reviews | New |
| | Spikes | New |
| Storyboarding | Storyboarding | Updated |
| Story Decomposition | Story Decomposition | Updated |
| Story Elaboration | Story Elaboration | Updated |
| Story Mapping | Story Mapping | Updated |
| User Story | User Stories | Updated |
| Value Stream Mapping | Value Stream Mapping | Updated |
| | Visioning | New |

CPSIA information can be obtained
at www.ICGtesting.com
Printed in the USA
LVOW06s2011161017

552665LV00005B/6/P